THE
SERMONS OF NESTORIUS

Nestorius,

Archbishop of Constantinople

Translated by: D.P. Curtin

Dalcassian Publishing Company
PHILADELPHIA, PA

THE SERMONS OF NESTORIUS

Copyright @ 2009 Dalcassian Publishing Company

All rights reserved. No part of this publication may be reproduced, distributed, or transmitted in any form or by any means, including photocopying, recording, or other electronic or mechanical methods, without the prior written permission of the publisher, except in the case of brief quotations embodied in critical reviews and certain other non-commercial uses permitted by copyright law. For permission request, write to Dalcassian Publishing Company at dalcassianpublishing at gmail.com

ISBN: 979-8-8690-2563-0 (Paperback)

Library of Congress Control Number:
Author: Curtin, D.P. (1985-)

Printed by Ingram Content Group, 1 Ingram Blvd, La Vergne, Tennessee

First printing edition 2009.

THE SERMONS OF NESTORIUS

THE SERMONS OF NESTORIUS

SERMON I.
The First Word of the Incarnation of our Lord Jesus Christ.

1. The doctrine of piety is the intention of the wise in the Church; but the doctrine of piety is the knowledge of providence: for he knows the providence of God, who knows God, the creator of bodies and souls. Therefore, as many as worship God without knowing this, it is evident that they are ignorant of the truth: for they confess that they know God, but deny it by deeds, as it is written (Tit. 1:16).

2. Now the creator must take care of those whom he has created.

3. Our life is unequal to the dignity of this great government. I imagine God as the workman in the mother's womb, and in those of the mother the

preservation of the secrets of my bowels is my first and greatest protection. I give birth and find sources of milk. I begin to have the work of cutting up the meat, and find myself armed with some knives, that is to say teeth. I act as a man, and a creature becomes a revenue to me: for below the earth feeds me, and from the sky the sun is kindled for me, the flowers give me springtime, summer brings me ears, winter brings forth rains, autumn depends on the tribute of wine.

4. What an unequal life we lead, consisting of poverty and riches! For not to be sustained would otherwise have been able to subsist. To see how great our protection is in these very things. The easy decay of corn compels the rich to sell to the needy for fear of corruption; the changeable nature of the wine compels the owner to enter into the trade in fear of loss. Therefore, gold is incorruptible and resistant to time, because nothing harms the poor when retained. For what evils eat at me, if they restrict their gold, when the rich are forced to sell the things that feed me?

5. The human race honored with ten thousand gifts was decorated with the last and closest gift of Incarnation Sunday. For since man is the image of the divine nature, the devil pushed and cast this into corruption. He grieved as if the king were his own image, and he renews the corrupted image, fashioning the nature of the Virgin without seed, just as Adam, who himself was formed without seed, works the restoration of the human race by man, since, he says, death by man, and the resurrection of the dead by man (1 Cor. 15:12).

6. Let those who are in the dispensation of Sunday's renewal the blind do not understand. neither what they speak, nor about whom they affirm (1 Tim. 1:7): who, as we have just learned, from we frequently ask each other whether Θεοτόκος should be called, that is, Mary, the mother of God, or mother of God, or ἀνθρωποτόκος, that is, the mother of man. Does God have a mother? Therefore, it is excusable that Gentiles subjugate the mothers of the gods. Therefore, Paul is a liar about the Deity of Christ, saying, ἀπάτωρ, ἀμήτωρ, ἄνευ γενεαλογίας (Heb. 7:3), that is, without father, without mother, without generation.

7. No, man very well, Mary gave birth to God. For that which is born of the flesh is flesh; and that of the spirit, is the spirit (John 3:6). The creature did not give birth to him who is uncreated; The Father did not beget God the Word from the Virgin: for in the beginning was the Word (John 1:1), as John

says. The creature did not give birth to the Creator but gave birth to man as an instrument of Deity; the Holy Spirit did not create God the Word: for that which is born of it is of the Holy Spirit (Matthew 1:20); but a temple was built for God the Word, that he might dwell from the Virgin.

8. God was indeed incarnate, but he did not die: but he raised him in whom he was incarnate; He was inclined to lift up that which fell, but he himself did not fall: the Lord looked down from heaven upon the children of men (Psal. 13:2); that is, bowing him to lift him who has fallen, as if he had fallen, he is to be blamed. God saw the fallen nature, and the power of the Deity grasped it, and lifted it up, holding, and remaining what he was, lifted him up high. For example, know what is said. If you wish to lift up a lying one, do you not touch the body with the body, and by conjoining yourself to it raise yourself up, and thus remain united to it as you were? so also esteem that sacrament of the Incarnation.

9. Because of the wearer of that garment which uses color; I worship because of the hidden that which is seen outside, inseparable from that which is outside God is the watcher.

10. How, then, of him who is not divided, honor and dignity dare to separate? I divide the natures but unite them in reverence.

11. Pay attention to what is being said. It is not by himself that God was formed in the womb: for if it were so, we should really be worshipers of man; but since God is in the assumed, from him who assumed he who was assumed was called, and He was called, and God is called.

12. God formed Dominic's incarnation. Let us fear the receptive form of God together and equally with that reverence for God the Word, as the truly inseparable image of the Divinity, as the image of the hidden judgment. Let us confess the duality, and worship it as: for one duality of natures is one because of unity. Hear Paul crying out both, that the eternity of the Only Begotten Deity, and the dignity of the partnership or conjunction, has become one: Jesus, says he, yesterday and today, he is the same for ever and ever. Amen (Heb. 13:8).

SERMON II.

On the dogma or Θεογνώσια, that is, on the unconfused conjunction of the two natures in Christ, and the communion of names, as in the Apollinarians. Cyril teaches the behavior in the church (Epistle to Acacius Melitenum): the title of the excerpts from the Council of Ephesus shows the inscription on dogma. By the name of dogma Θεογνωσίαν is to be understood, and so the knowledge of the humanity at the same time and the Divinity of Christ, says the beginning. A series of parts, not invented by us for discretion, but easily known to be true, if anyone has put together the places from which each one is taken.

I do not prove our devotion to myself by cries; but I praise the desire concerning the dogmas, and that you remember the Lord's Deity and humanity.

And after a little: I observe that the people possess much reverence and a most prudent piety; but ignorance blinds Θεογνωσίας. But this is not the crime of the people; but I should say with shame, because the teachers have not had time to give you anything clearer and clearer even about dogmas.

But you remember exactly what I have often said to you, when I distinguished two natures in Christ the Lord: for there are two, if you look at nature; if the dignity, simple. For the authority of nature is one, because of conjunction; natures, indeed, always standing in their own order, but united by dignity, as I have already said, into a single authority.

For this reason, I want to favor you more cautiously, or to applaud you: there is no division, nor conjunction, nor power, nor sonship, nor of this, which is Christ. In these there is no division; there is indeed a division in Godhead and humanity. Christ, according as he is Christ, is undivided; and the Son, inasmuch as he is the Son, is undivided. For we do not have two Christs or two sons; nor is Christ the first and the second among us; neither one and the other; nor again another Son, and again another Son; but he himself is double, not by dignity, but by nature.

But as we say, God is the maker of all things, and God is Moses: for God, he says, I have made you Pharaoh (Exodus 7:1); and Israel the Son of God: for the Son, he says, is my firstborn Israel (Exodus 4:22); and just as we say the Christ Saul: No, he says, I will lay my hand on him, because he is the Christ of the Lord (1 Kings 24:7); likewise Cyrus: These things saith the Lord unto my Christ Cyrus (Isaiah 45:1); and the holy Babylon: For I, he says, command the sanctified ones, and I lead them (Isaiah 13:3); thus we say Lord, and Christ, and God, and Son, and holy; but the communion of names is indeed similar, but the dignity is not the same.

Whenever, therefore, the Holy Scripture is to say, either the generation of Christ from the blessed Virgin, or death, it never says God, but either Christ, or Jesus, or the Lord; since these three natures indicate two natures, just this, just that, just both. But it is such that I say, whenever the Scripture mentions to us the generation from the Virgin, what does it say? God sent his Son (Gal. 4:4); He does not say: God sent the Word; but he uses that name because it indicates two natures. For because the Son is man and God, he says: God sent his Son made of woman; so that when you hear, made of a woman, you immediately consider the name given, which indicates two natures; and the generation from the blessed Virgin of the Son. For the Virgin Χριστοτόκος gave birth to the Son of God: for since the Son of God is twofold in nature, she indeed gave birth to the Son of God, because she gave birth to man, who is the Son of God, because of the Son of God conjoined to him.

We have made it clear that the divine Scripture gives the name of the Son at the birth of Christ's mother, the Virgin. Hear now even in death and see where the name of God is finally placed, that we may introduce a suffering God. When we were enemies, he says, we were reconciled to God through the death of his Son (Rom. 5:10); He does not say, by the death of the Word of God.

God was indeed the Word before the incarnation, and the Son, and God with the Father; indeed, in the latter times he took the form of a servant: but since he was previously the Son, and is so called after the assumption, he cannot be called a divided Son, lest we establish two sons. but because he was conjoined to him, who was from the beginning the Son, he cannot receive a division according to the dignity of sonship. As to the dignity of filiation, I say, not as to natures; therefore, also God the Word is called Christ, because he has a perpetual conjunction with Christ; nor does it happen that God the Word does anything without humanity; for it was brought to the highest conjunction, but not to deification, as the wise among the more recent dogmatists assert.

Thus, also Christ according to the flesh, because of the conjunction which he has with God the Word, we call God, knowing that he is a man who appears. Listen to Paul preaching both: From the Jews, he says, Christ according to the flesh, who is above all gods (Rom. 9:5). First, he confesses to man, then, in conjunction with God, he says that God is the one who appears, lest anyone think that man's Christianity is a knife.

Hear also this name, Lord, sometimes of Christ's humanity, sometimes of his divinity, sometimes of both. Every time you eat the bread and drink the cup, you will announce the Lord's death (1 Cor. 11:26). Hear from those who objected to the incompetence of those who went before, that they read that this mystery was of the greatest benefit, and that the commemoration of it should bring to men; and listen not to me saying this, but to blessed Paul: As often as you eat this bread; He did not say, every time you eat this Divinity, but every time you eat this bread. See that the body of Dominic was proposed to him: As often as you eat this bread, of which the body itself is the antitype. Let us see then whose death as often as you eat this bread and drink this cup, you will proclaim the Lord's death. Listen in more detail below until it comes. But who will come? They will see the Son of Man coming in the clouds of heaven with great glory (Matthew 24:30). And what is greater, before the apostles the prophet shows that he is coming more clearly, and cries out about the Jews, saying: They will see whom they have reproached (Zech. 12:10). So what is their regret? It is not God's side, but man's.

Let us therefore keep the conjunction of natures unconfused; let us confess God in man; let us worship the man to be worshiped by a certain divine conjunction with God almighty.

Say about assuming that there is a God; add from the assumption that the form of a servant; bring forth afterwards the dignity of conjunction, that the authority of the two be common, that the dignity of the two be the same; and remaining natures, confess unity.

SERMON III.

The behavior of Nestorius, as it were, against the Arians and Macedonians, against the Catholics who defended the true union of natures in Christ. Inventing a greater injury to Christ, they dissect the Holy Spirit from the divine nature, which shaped his humanity in the Virgin's womb: For what, says the Scripture, was born in her, is of the Holy Spirit (Matt. 1:20); who reformed according to the righteousness which was figured: For, he says, that which was manifest in the flesh was justified in the spirit (1 Tim. 3:16); who made him terrible and formidable to demons: For I, he says, cast out demons in the Spirit of God (Luke 11:20); whose flesh is made a temple: For I saw a spirit, he says, descending like a dove, and abiding on him (John 1:32); who granted him ascension into heaven: for, as the Scripture says, he commanded the apostles whom he had chosen by the Holy Spirit, and was lifted up into heaven (Acts 1:32). Here, I say, the Spirit who gave so great glory is claimed by these to be the servant of Christ.

But how can he be a servant who cooperates with the Son and the Father? For if anyone seeks the works of the Spirit, he will find them neither distant nor unlike the works of the Father and the Son; not because the one Deity is divided, but because the divine Scripture disperses those things which are of one power into individual substances, so that the similitude of the Trinity may be shown. Consider this, beginning with the works done in his time: God the Word became flesh and dwelt among us (John 1:14). Consider the man the Father has taken for himself: for the Lord said to my Lord: Sit at my right hand (Ps. 19:1). The Spirit glorified him who was taken up: For when the Spirit of truth comes, he himself will glorify me (John 16:4).

Do you want us to add to these another efficiency of the Trinity? The Son dwelt in the body. The Father recommended the baptized. He formed him in the Virgin Spirit. The Son chose the apostles: I, he says, chose you (John 15:19). The Father sanctified: Father, he says, sanctify them in your truth (John 17:17). The Spirit made the speakers (Acts 2:4).

And indeed these (the Arians), although they deride the Word as a lesser God in the majesty of the paternal Deity, yet admit that He is not a new one: but these also pronounce Him to be second and posterior to the blessed Mary, and consign Him to the temporal mother of the workman of the times to the Divinity; indeed, they do not even admit that He is the mother of Christ. For if it was not man's nature, but God the Word, whom she gave birth to, what she gave birth to, by no means is the mother of him who was born; for how will his mother become something, who is by nature a stranger to the mother? But if the true mother is called by them; therefore, he who is published is not the nature of Divinity, but man; indeed, it is the property of every mother's consubstantial to obey her.

Therefore, she will not be a mother who has not at all given birth to her consubstantial. Therefore, because she is called a mother by them, she gave birth to him who is similar in substance. But who will be like him according to her substance? Without a doubt he existed by the work of the Holy Spirit. For what is born in her is of the Holy Spirit (Matt. 1:20); with whom the Word God was incessantly.

Therefore, the Word God was not born of Mary, but remained in him who was born of her. He did not begin with the Virgin but was inseparably associated at all times with him who, growing up through the months, was gradually composed in the Virgin's womb. But it is another thing to say: He who was born remains with him; and another thing, that he who remains with the new-born, is the one to whom a month would have been needed in order to be born.

When Nestorius in the midst of the profane church was using new words (with which he was attacking both Θεοτόκον and the twin birth of Christ), a certain man of course who was honest, who was still among the laity, but who had nevertheless gathered an admirable learning for himself, moved by a fervent and religious zeal, and exclaiming with a more contentious voice: He says that centuries ago the Word also underwent a second generation, that is, that according to the flesh, and from a woman. When these people were tumultuous, and the greater and saner part of them were extolling him with the greatest praises, as being pious and wise in the first place, and unexperienced in the correct doctrines, others nevertheless raised against him, he himself (Nestorius) intervened, and soon approved of those whom he had lost by his teaching. moreover, he sharpened his tongue against him who had not supported his dogmas, and against the holy Fathers who had established for us the pious definition of faith, and said:

I am glad to see your zeal: for now and then things can be plainly reproved, which have been maliciously said by an unhappy man. For those of whom there are two generations, their two children must necessarily be; but the Church recognizes only one Son, the Lord Christ himself.

But we must know that which has just come to the remembrance of the council of Nicaea, that it never dared to say that the Word God was born of the virgin Mary; for he says: We believe in one Father Almighty, and in one Lord Jesus Christ. Pay attention to the fact that when the Fathers first established Christ, which shows the conjunction of two natures, they did not say, one God, the Word; but they received a name which signified both, that when descending, when you hear of death, you are not troubled by any newness, and when you are crucified and buried, as the divinity so patient, you are not hurt by the hearing.

Next, let's see what they are subscribing to. We also believe in one Lord Jesus Christ, the only begotten of the Father, who came down for us and was incarnated by the Holy Spirit. They did not say that he was born of the Holy Spirit. See how they interpret it by going down, because they said that man was made. God, they say, we say incarnate, not showing the changeability of the divine nature taking on flesh, but the indwelling which He carried out in man.

And after a while: Retain this, because, omitting to say: We believe in God the Word, his only begotten Son, they said: We believe in one Lord Jesus Christ, consubstantial with the Father, true God from true God, through whom all things were made, who came down for us men and our salvation , and was incarnated by the Holy Spirit, from the virgin Mary, and became man. They said nowhere, he was born. Why, we think? That they should not introduce two births of Divinity.

And after a while: for thus the Scripture says: God sent his Son, made of a woman, made under the law (Gal. 4:4). Here indeed he shows two natures. But what happens only around man, he narrates. Require certainly from the litigant who is made under the law. The word God? Not at all.

So, what were we saying? Do not be afraid to accept Mary as your spouse; for what is born (whether we say born or done, nothing harms the sense), for what is born in it, is from the Holy Spirit (Matt. 10:20). If we say that God the Word was born in the womb (for it is one thing to be at the same time as being born, another thing to be born), for that which was born in it, he says, is from the Holy Spirit, that is, the Holy Spirit created what is in it. The Fathers therefore saw, as they were acquainted with the Holy Scriptures, that if we say that He who was incarnate was born, then God the Word, the Son of the Holy Spirit, will be found to have two Fathers. But if we say the fact, it will be found that God the Word is a creature of the Holy Spirit. Fleeing therefore the expression of generation, they said thus: He came down for our salvation and was incarnate. What is it then, to be incarnate? He was not converted from Divinity into flesh.

In what they said, incarnate from the Holy Spirit, they followed the evangelist: for when the evangelist had come to ἐνανθρώπησιν, he fled to speak of generation from the Word, and said incarnation. Listen: And the Word was made flesh (John 1:14); He did not say: The Word was made flesh. For when either the apostles or the evangelists make mention of the Son, they say that he was born of a woman. Notice, please, that when they say the name of the Son, that which was born, they say that he was born of a woman. But where they make mention of the Word, no one dares to say generation by humanity. Hear blessed John the Evangelist, when he came to the Word and its ἐναθρώπησιν. Hear what he says: The Word became flesh; that is, he assumed flesh; and he dwelt among us; that is, it puts on our nature. And we saw the glory of the Son himself; He did not say: We have seen the generation of the Word.

And after a while: For if indeed they had said: We believe in one God the Word, it would have been the case that death would be attributed to the divine nature; therefore, they take a common name, namely, Jesus Christ, in order to signify both that he is dead and that he is not dead. And so it is just as if someone says, that man is dead, although the soul is immortal; yet because he said the name which signifies two natures, the body which dies, and the immortal soul, therefore there is no danger in that word; for both are called man, and body, and soul. Thus, also said that great choir about Christ.

The symbol of Nicaea, which is also that of Constantinople. We believe in one God, the Father Almighty, creator of all things visible and invisible.

And in one Lord Jesus Christ, the only begotten Son of God, begotten of the Father, that is, of the substance of the Father, God from God, light from light, true God from true God, not begotten, consubstantial with the Father:

through whom all things were made, and things in heaven, and things on earth.

He came down for us men, and for our salvation, and was incarnated, and became man, and suffered, and rose again on the third day; ascended into heaven, to come to judge the living and the dead.

And into the Holy Spirit. But those who say: There was a time when he was not, and before he was born, he was not; the Catholic and Apostolic Church anathematized these. The symbol of Antioch. I believe in the one and only true God, the Almighty Father, creator of all visible and invisible creatures.

And into our Lord Jesus Christ, his only begotten Son, and the firstborn of all creation, born of him before all ages, and not made, true God from true God, ὁμοούσιον the Father, by whom the ages were joined together, and all things were made. He who came for us, and was born of the virgin Mary, and was crucified under Pontius Pilate, and was buried, and rose again on the third day according to the Scriptures, and ascended into heaven, and will come again to judge the living and the dead.

The Letter of Marius the Merchant

On the difference between the heresy of Nestorius and the dogmas of Paul of Samosate, Ebion, Photinus, and Marcellus. Marius Mercator, servant of Christ, greetings to my fellow reader.

1. This doctrine of Paul and Nestorius of Samosata is no less impious than vain. Nestorius writes about the Word of God, not indeed as Paul feels, who defines it as the efficacious Word, not the substantive, but the extension of the power of God. Yet, Nestorius does not confess that the same is true of the substantive Word, that He is naturally the Son of God; but he says, indeed, wittily, because he does not express it, that there is no Son from eternity, but only the Word, that, remaining in the substance of the Father, God is consubstantial, which the Greeks say ὁμοούσιον; But he asserts that he is and ought to be called the Son, who was born of Mary.

2. And thus he divides the eternal from the temporal; deputing the things of majesty to God and the Word of God and deputing to the other the things of human weakness: and because of his individuality and inseparable connection he was worthy of the denomination of the Son of God, indeed he who has this very thing by merit, and by adoption, not by nature.

3. It is indeed objected to him by the Catholics, why by this sense two should think of Christs and two Sons, he himself answers thus: I, he says, define one Christ, who is to be said to be anointed by chrism; that this very Son of God is one, because he was joined to God the Word by an indivisible partnership; sometimes because of this very inseparable conjunction, or connection, even that Word is conjoined with the same surnames, which are completely alien to its nature; finally, by virtue of this Jesus Christ's unique birth and incomparable life, he was held to be worthy, like a temple, in all the fullness of his divinity, and to be inhabited by this God and the Word of God.

4. In that, then, he is joined to Paul of Samosate, in which he separates the inhabitant and the habitation according to their merits, dividing what is proper to each of them, from the diversity of nature, which indeed they both have in common with Ebion, and Photinus, and Galata Marcellus.

5. In the fact that he confesses the substantial Word of God and asserts that God is from eternity with the Father, he rightly disagrees with those mentioned, and is joined to the right faith. 6. But again the same Word says that God is not naturally the Son of God the Father, but only the Word, as we explained above, and in Christ the Lord he divides the merits of each one's substance, he incurs the great crime of impiety, and hence he is condemned by law as an alien and a pervert from the ecclesiastical faith.

Homily of Proclus.

By the bishop of Cyzicus, given by Nestorius sitting in the great church of Constantinople, on the incarnation of our Lord Jesus Christ, that Deipara be the blessed virgin Mary, and born of her, not only God, nor pure man, but Emmanuel, unmistakably and unchangeably God and man.

1. Today, virginal solemnity calls our tongue, brothers, into a proclamation, and the present festival is made as a provider of utility to those who have assembled, and very competently. For it has the substance of chastity, and the glory of the female sex, because of her who is in time a mother, and always a virgin.

2. For behold, both the earth and the sea offer gifts to the Virgin; and these, directing the footsteps of the climbers without hindrance. Let nature rejoice, let women be honored, let humanity lead the chorus, let virgins be glorified: For where sin abounded, grace abounded more (Rom. 5:20). Blessed Mary has summoned us, the immaculate vessel of virginity, the paradise of the rational second Adam, the worker of the union of natures, the solemnity of the healthy exchange, the bush which the fire of the divine birth did not burn, the truly light cloud which carried him who is above the cherubim with his body. Oh, the purest wool of the heavenly rains, from which the shepherd is clothed with sheep!

3. Mary, mother and handmaid, Virgin and heaven, the only bridge of God to men, the terrible fabric of the dispensation, in which is woven the tunic of the ineffable incarnation, the superweaver of whose work is the Holy Spirit; the weaver, the overshadowing virtue of the highest; and the garment, the ancient garment of Adam; tufts, from the immaculate flesh of the Virgin; the ray, the immeasurable grace of the wearer; an artist, that through obedience he leapt upon the Word. Who has seen, who has heard, because God dwelt uncircumcised in the womb, and whom heaven could not take, the womb of the Virgin took.

4. God was born of a woman, but not naked; and he was born a man, but not pure; and he who was born through the gate of old sin shows the gate of salvation: for where the serpent poured out poison through disobedience, there the Word, entering through obedience, fashioned the temple life-giving.

Whence Cain, the first disciple of sin, emerged, from whence Christ, the savior of our race, sprouted without seed.

5. The lover of men was not ashamed of women's births, for life was the business that was transacted. He was not defiled by the habitation of the entrails, which he himself had prepared without reproach. If the mother did not remain a virgin, the man who was born is pure, and there was no miraculous birth; but if she remained a virgin even after childbirth, he was ineffably born of her, who entered without prohibition through closed doors, and Thomas, recognizing the conjunction of his natures, cried out, saying: My Lord and my God (John 20:28).

6. Do not be ashamed, O man, of childbirth, for he has become for us the occasion of salvation. If he had not been born of a woman, he would not have died; if he did not die, he would by no means destroy by death him who has the power of death (Heb. 2:14), that is, the devil. It is no injury to the architect to remain in what he has built; He does not pollute the potter reviving the clay which he had fashioned: so he does not pollute the uncontaminated proceeding from the Virgin's womb; for while he was forming it, he was not defiled, nor was he defiled when he passed through it.

7. O use, in which the guarantee of common liberty is composed! O belly, in which weapons are made against death! O field, in which nature's farmer Christ, like a spike, sprouted without seed! Oh, the temple in which God became a priest, not changing nature, but wearing him who is according to the order of Melchizedek, because of mercy!

8. The Word was made flesh (John 1:14), although the Jews do not believe in the birth. God is clothed in the form of a man, even though the heathen deceives him by a miracle: for this is the offense of the Jews, and the foolishness of the Gentiles (1 Cor. 1:23) is a mystery, because a miracle is beyond reason. If the Word had not dwelt in the womb, the flesh would not have sat on the throne. If it were an offense to God to enter the womb, and it were an offense to the angels to minister to men.

9. He who is according to nature, as God, ἀπαθὴς, because of mercy became πολιπαθής. God did not become Christ from advancement, he is far away, but because of compassion, as we believe, he became man. We do not preach a

deified man, but we confess God incarnate. He enlisted his own maidservant, his mother. He who is essentially without a mother is, according to the dispensation, without a father: for how is he, according to Paul, without a father and without a mother (Heb. 7:3)? If a man is pure, he is not without a mother; if God is naked, he is not without a father: but now he is the same, indeed without a mother as the molder; but without a father, as he was formed.

10. Be ashamed of the appeal of the archangel, O man; he who evangelized Mary is called Gabriel. But what does Gabriel mean? God and man. The appeal preceded that the dispensation might be believed.

11. Learn the cause of the presence and glorify the power of the incarnate. The human race owed much and failed to meet the debt. Through Adam we recorded every sin, and the devil kept us slaves: he brought out our instruments, using his many-patient body for papers: the evil counterfeiter of passions stood striking the debt against us, and demanding judgment. It was therefore necessary that one of the two, or that death be brought forth by judgment, because all have sinned; or such compensation should be given as would justify the whole repetition. And indeed, man could not save, for he was subject to debt: the angel was not able to redeem, for he failed in the price of deliverance; He who was without sin had to die for sinners: for this alone is the only solution left to evil.

12. What then? He who from nothing had brought all nature to be, who was deficient in no gift of goodness, found, and having been condemned to death, the most certain life, and the most decent solution to death: for he becomes a man, as he himself knows (for the word cannot be interpreted as a miracle), and he dies thereby. that he became man; and by that he frees that which existed before, according to Paul saying: In whom we have redemption, through his blood the remission of sins (Eph. 1:7).

13. O wonderful things! He traded immortality for others, for he himself was immortal. for such another, according to the dispensation, neither was, nor was, nor is, nor will be, he is the only one who was born of the Virgin, God and man, not only that which can be contrasted for appreciation, having a dignity compared to a multitude of criminals, but superior to all judgments. In this, indeed, that he was the Son, preserving that which is unchangeable to the Father; but in this that which is a founder, that which is of virtue, having

indefatigably; in that he who loves to be pitied, those things which are of compassion, without any taxing contribution; in fine, in that which is a priest, offering that which was suitable for representation: to which no one will find anything like, or a neighbor at any time in any.

14. Pay attention to his love for people. Voluntarily adjudged to death, he dissolved death, which was against those who crucified him, and turned the iniquity of those who perished into the salvation of the unrighteous.

15. Therefore it was not for a pure man to save, in fact he also needed a savior, according to Paul saying: For all have sinned and stand in need of the glory of God (Rom. 3:28). Indeed, because sin delivered a guilty man to the devil, the devil acted as a handover to death: those around us were in great danger, and the solution of death was impossible.

16. Those who were sent for the doctors accused; what then? When the prophets saw that the wound was beyond human skill, they cried out to the heavenly physician: and he indeed said: Lord, bow down your heavens and come down (Ps. 143:5). Another: Heal me, O Lord, and I will be healed (Jer. 17:14). Another cried: Arouse thy power, and come, that we may be set free (Ps. 79:3). Another said: Alas for me! my soul, because the merciful perished from the earth. Another said: If indeed God dwelt with men. Another: May your mercy seize us quickly, Lord. Also, another: God, attend to my helper, O Lord, to help me quickly (Ps. 69, 2). Another: He who is about to come will come and will not delay (Habakkuk 2:3). Another: I went astray like a sheep that had perished; seek your servant (Ps. 118, 176).

17. He therefore did not despise the oppression of human nature, who by nature exists as king and God; but he who was ever present came, and paid the ransom with his own blood, and gave for the human race a reparation for death, which was clothed with a body from the Virgin, and redeemed the world from the curse of the law. hence Paul cries out: Christ has redeemed us from the curse of the law (Gal. 3:13).

18. He, therefore, who redeems us, is not a pure man, O Jews: for the nature of men served sin; but neither was God naked, for he had a body, O Manichaeus, for unless he had clothed me, he would not have saved me; but he who had taken the sentence in the Virgin's womb was clothed with guilt,

and there a terrible exchange took place: for, having given the Spirit, He took flesh, He was the same with the Virgin and from the Virgin; and the Spirit indeed overshadowed her, but he himself became flesh from her.

19. If one is Christ and the other is God the Word, there will no longer be a trinity, but a quaternity. Do not tear apart the tunic of dispensation, which is woven from above, do not be a disciple of Arius; he impiously divides the essence, you do not divide the unity, so that you are not divided from God.

20. Say, who appeared to those sitting in darkness and in the shadow of death (Luke 1:79)? Man? And how, if he dwelt in darkness, according to Paul saying: Who delivered us from the power of darkness (Col. 1, 13); and again: For you were sometimes in darkness (Ephesians 5:8). Who, then, is enlightened? Let David teach you, saying: God is the Lord, and he has given us light (Ps. 177:27); they came together in nature, and the unity remained unconfused.

21. He came to save, but he also had to suffer: how then could both be done? A pure man was not able to save, a naked God could not suffer, God Himself existing by nature, became man, and by what He really was He saved; but he endured what he had become.

22. Therefore, when the Church saw that the Synagogue had crowned him with thorns, he lamented the presumption and said: Daughters of Jerusalem, come out and see the crown with which his mother crowned him (Cant. 3:11); for he himself bore a crown of thorns, that he might dissolve the opinion of the thorns; himself in the bosom of the Father and in the womb of the Virgin, between the elbows of the mother and on the wings of the winds: he was worshiped above by the angels, and below he reclined with the curtains: they did not look at the Seraphim out of reverence, and Pilate questioned him: the servant was beaten, and the creature was held: he was nailed to the cross, and the throne of glory was not naked: it lay in the sepulcher, and spread heaven like a skin: it was counted among the dead, and it plundered hell: it was slandered below as a seducer, and glorified by the saints above. O wonderful mystery!

23. I see miracles, and I preach divinity: I look at sufferings, and I do not deny humanity; but Emmanuel indeed opened the gates of nature, as a man;

but the virgin does not break the barrier, as God does; but thus, he came out of the womb, as he entered by hearing. Thus, was he born, how was he conceived; He entered incorruptible, he came out incorruptible, according to the prophet Ezekiel saying: The Lord turned me to the way of the outer gate of the sanctuary, which looks towards the East, and this was closed. And the Lord said to me: Son of man, that gate shall be shut, and shall not be opened: no one shall pass through it, but only the Lord God shall enter, and it shall be shut (Ezek. 44:1).

24. Behold the manifest approval of Mary, the holy mother of God, let every contradiction be dissolved henceforth, and let us be enlightened by the doctrine of the holy Scriptures, that we may obtain the kingdom of heaven in Christ Jesus our Lord, to whom be glory forever and ever. Amen.

SERMON IV.

Of the incarnation. Who was the first and extemporaneous to address Proclus in a panegyric speech to the Virgin Θεοτόκον.

1. It is not to be wondered that the people who love Christ should give applause to those who spend the service of speaking for the blessed Mary: for this very thing has become a temple Sunday's flesh, exceeds all that is worthy of praise. But your amiability must focus on that, so as not to do more than is necessary or appropriate to turn around the honor and praise of that blessed one, we should seem to confound the dignity of the Word of God, who was twice begotten by making him. And in order that you may understand the matter, let us use simpler language, and use speech that is easiest for everyone to understand, so that what is said does not exceed what is heard by the listeners.

2. He who says simply that God was born of Mary, first of all prostitutes the nobility of all things to the nations with dogmas, and when he exposes it to the middle, he sets it up to be reproached and laughed at; for at once the heathen, accepting with censure, because God was born of Mary, will bring it against the Christian: for necessarily he who says simply God born of Mary, and not him who was born, by the conjunction of two natures, that is to say divine and human, God he will hear: I do not want to worship a God who was born and died and was buried. Now the liquid division of the dogma is this: He who was born, and lived through the seasons of growth, and was carried in the womb during the legitimate months, here has a human nature, but of course joined to God.

3. But it is another thing to say that God who is the Word of the Father, which is most liquid and firm and irreproachable to the Gentiles, was conjoined to the one who was born of Mary. and another thing, because the Divinity itself needed a birth running in months: for the Word, the God of times, is a workman, not fashioned in time.

4. I was therefore very surprised at the division of the previous teacher on this point, who said (Part 3): He who was born of a woman is neither a naked God nor a pure man; because it is not necessary to say that God is naked and in any way generated: for no one who is older generates himself; nor again is

it to be professed that humanity is naked, but that humanity is united to God and generated.

5. I want you to be drawn into that, who are keen examiners of religion (for I have this opinion of you as well as of the Antiochenes); therefore, as I said, I want you to be drawn into that, because God has become a priest, I cannot bear it ; for if God is a workman and a priest, whose delegation must be presented by the priests?

6. I said these things for your love, and I would have said more, had it not entered my mind, that I seem to be arguing against the teachers of the Church. I want you, therefore, to be perceptive in examining dogmas, and neither to confuse the humanity received from the Word of God, nor to call a naked man that which is born; but neither has God the Word, tempered or mixed, lost his proper essence.

7. For this reason, when the disciples were astonished, at the time when he was taken up into heaven, and with him, as far as we can imagine, considering this: do you think that human nature has been resolved? Do you think that in the heavens it remains in the same essence? And the angels coming to them, amazed at this vision, said: This Jesus who is seen, this one who needed the increase of the month, this one who died, this one who endured the cross, so will he come as you saw him ascending into heaven (Acts 1:11). And again, the blessed Paul in the Acts of the Apostles: In the man, he says, in whom God decided to judge the world of the earth, giving faith to all, raising him from the dead (Ibid. 17:31). Did God the Word rise from the dead? But if the giver of life has been put to death, who will be the one who gives life?

8. Apart from this, we are also very reprehensible to the Arians; for if in any way he was born and let us simply call God the Word, see what is made of this. You say simply: God is the one who was born of Mary, immediately the heretic accuses us: therefore, you undeservedly accuse us, saying that the Son is a lesser one and created by the Father; since with you this is also in the confession, saying that the Word is God who was born of Mary.

9. Hear what the same God the Word testifies about himself: Go tell my brothers: I go to my Father and your Father, my God and your God (John 20:17). But when he said this, he who was born of the blessed Mary, was

indeed consubstantial with us in humanity; but in that which is joined to God, was far from ours, because God is a better substance.

10. Then you will be freed from their blasphemy: and you will easily and briefly proclaim the sacrament of religion in this way: Indeed, another God is the Word, who was in the temple, which the Spirit worked, and another temple besides the indwelling God. The temple is dissolved by death; But it is proper for him who dwells in the temple to rise again. This is not my speech, but the voice of the Lord: Loosen this temple, he says, and in three days I will raise it up (John 2:19).

11. Therefore let us confess the unity of conjunction, but natures and substances are twofold, otherwise the Word will be found to be a creature of the Holy Spirit: for what does the evangelist say? That which is born in her is of the Holy Spirit (Matthew 1:20). But if the Word God was naked and alone, nor, as the evangelist says, the Spirit created his temple in the blessed Mary, will God be found the Word of the Holy Spirit's workman.

12. Let us therefore avoid the error of this confusion: let us say that our Lord Christ, according to his nature, is twofold; according to which the Son is one.

13. But I, who reported this to me, often laughed with joy, because, they say, the bishop is wise in the things of Photius, not knowing either what they speak, or about whom they affirm (1 Tim. 1, 7); for this which is said by, Photini, dogmatism is found overthrown. For Photinus' sense gives the beginning of the Word to God from the birth of Mary, saying that the Word God always existed before the ages.

14. For them, let the proverbial word suffice for me: Do not answer the imprudent according to his imprudence (Prov. 26:4). But I want you, as perspicacious examiners of dogmas, not to use applause, not to be attracted by allurements of speech, or anything of dogma, and to think that the examined reason is a presumption of novelty, but to judge it rather the glory of truth.

SERMON V.

On the God born and the Virgin Θεοτόκω, who is the second against Proclus.

1. I have often asked those who defend Θεοτόκον: Do you say that the Deity was born of the holy Virgin? At these words they immediately retorted: Is there anyone, they say, who suffers from such a disease of blasphemy, as to say that what gave birth to the temple, the work of the Holy Spirit, God himself created in it? Then when I submit to these things: What, then, is absurdly said by us, when we are indeed advised to bring forth this voice, but to proceed to the common signification of the two natures? But then they think that it is blasphemous that we say: Either to confess openly the Divinity born of the blessed Mary; or, if you shun this voice as blasphemous, why do you say the same thing as I pretend not to say it?

2. If you were to pronounce Deipara with simple faith, there would be no envy of speech in me seeking the meaning of the word; but because I see that you, under the pretext of honoring the blessed Mary, confirm the blasphemy of the heretics, therefore I cautiously guard against the utterance of the saying, since I suspect a danger lurking in that saying.

3. That I may say this more clearly, and that it may be more easily understood by men, those who followed Arius, and Eunomius, and Apollinarius, and all the men of this kind, endeavored to bring in the appellation of Θεοτόκου, as having been effected by a mixture of two natures not at all distinct, nothing of these that which is more inferior should be accepted as a matter of humanity; and a place would already be open to them against the Divinity itself, as if all things were said of one, not by reason of the dignity resulting from the conjunction itself, but by reason of its own nature. For there is one Christ, and one Lord; but in Christ, the only-begotten, I say, the Son, and the name of Christ and of the Son is said now of divinity, now of humanity and divinity.

4. I have already said many times: If anyone among you who is simpler, or among any others, rejoices in this voice of Θεότοκος, with me there is no envy of the voice, so long as he does not make the Virgin a goddess.

5. If God is Christ, they say, and Christ was born of the blessed Mary, why is not the Virgin the mother of God? Nothing hidden, which is objected to by them. For the lover of truth accepts and objects to everything that can be said of falsity. A child is formed in the womb, but in so far as it has received a form, it does not yet have a soul: but when it has been formed, the soul is already formed by God. Therefore, as a woman gives birth to a body, but God gives a soul; nor therefore shall a woman be called the begetter of the soul, because she gave birth to an animal, but rather the begetter of man: so also the blessed Virgin, though she gave birth to a man, at the same time passing through the Word of God, is not therefore the begetter of God: for the divinity of the Word did not begin with the blessed Virgin, but was God's nature.

6. Of blessed John the Baptist it is preached by the holy angels, that the infant must be filled with the Holy Spirit, still from his mother's womb (Luke 1:15); and thus blessed John the Baptist was delivered having the Holy Spirit. What then? Will you call Elizabeth herself the progenitor of the Spirit? Return your attention to this, and if there are any among you who are moved by what is being said, as if it were unheard of and unusual, forgive their ignorance.

7. Hear also another testimony of theirs, for if they had known, they would never have crucified the Lord of glory. Behold the Lord of glory, he says. He does not thus address humanity, but Divinity; but this is what separates that most union of men: for when you say that this is not the Lord, but that he is, you make Christ a naked man. What then do you say under the ecclesiastical person, heretic? Is the Lord himself also a man, or otherwise? If it is the Lord, they communicate with each other what is said. If not, don't you, when you make Christ a naked and simple man, impose this shame on me. Let us hear the blessed Paul crying out openly who it is that was crucified. Listen therefore to his voice very clearly: Indeed, he was crucified because of infirmity, but he lives because of the power of God. If he was crucified because of infirmity, who was infirm, heretical? Is God the Word?

8. See what happens, heretics. I do not envy the name of the Virgin Χριστοτόκῳ: for I admit that she who conceived God is to be revered; through which the Lord of all will pass; through which the sun of justice shone forth: for God was the Word, and conjoined with man, and dwelling in him; but further I suspect the applause. How did you understand what I said? I did not say he passed, for what he was born for: for I do not so easily forget

my opinion. I was taught by Scripture that God passed through the Virgin Χριστοτόκον; I was born, not educated.

9. Nowhere does the divine Scripture assert that God was born of the Virgin Χριστοτόκῳ; but Jesus Christ, the Son, the Lord. Let us all confess this: for what the divine Scriptures have taught, he who does not immediately receive is miserable. Arise, take the child and his mother (Matthew 2:13). This is the voice of the angels, even yours. Perhaps the archangel knew his generation. Arise, and take the child and his mother; He did not say: Arise and receive God and his mother.

SERMON VI.

Concerning the sayings of the Apostle's Epistle to the Hebrews: Consider the apostle and priest of our confession, Jesus, etc. (Heb. 3:1).

1. When they hear the name of the apostle in Christ, they misunderstand the word of God to be an apostle. When they also read the term priest, they imagine that God is the priest, a strange madness. For who, hearing the office of the apostle, does not at once see that a man is pointed out? Who, hearing the name of the high priest, calls the nature of the Divinity to the service of the priest?

2. For if God is a high priest, who is it that should be worshiped by his office? If God is going to offer sacrifices as a priest, there will be no one to whom God is to be offered. For what is he worthy of the Divinity, if he should offer sacrifices to a superior as if he were inferior?

3. Where, then, did the priest appear to them to be called God, who, according to the rite of the priesthood, does not at all need a sacrifice for his advancement? for he is a perpetual possessor of Divinity. Namely, the priest, chosen from among men, and accepted, is appointed by God for men (Heb. 5:1).

4. He did not seize the angels, but the seed of Abraham (Heb. 2:16). Are you the seed of Abraham, the Divinity itself? Hear also the following voice: Wherefore he had to become like his brothers in all things (Ibid., 17). Is it Divinity? For what brothers could God the Word have like himself?

5. Look also at what is added to these sayings: That he might become a merciful and faithful priest to God; for in that in which he suffered and was himself tempted, he can also help those who are tempted (Ibid., 18). He, therefore, who suffered, is a merciful priest; but it is the temple that is tolerable, not this one who is the giver of life, God.

6. Abraham's seed is he who was yesterday and today, according to the voice of the apostle Paul (Heb. 13:8); not he who said: Before Abraham was, I am

(John 8:58). He is like the brothers in all things (Hebrews 2:17); he who accepted the brotherhood of the human soul and body, not he who said: He who sees me sees my Father also (John 14:9).

7. And he was sent, consubstantial with us, and anointed, and preaching release to the captives, and sight to the blind: for the Spirit of the Lord is upon me, because of that he anointed me; He sent me to preach good news to the poor, to heal the brokenhearted, to preach release to the captives and sight to the blind (Isaiah 61:1).

8. When he further said of Christ that he had been sent to announce the release of the captives; The apostle added this also and said: He who is faithful to God has become a priest (Hebrews 2:17). For it was done here, it had not been perpetually before. Here he gradually advanced in rank among the priests, heretical. Hear the voice declaiming this more clearly to you: He who, in the days of his flesh, offered prayers and supplications to him who could save him from death, with a strong cry and tears, was heard for his reverence; and indeed, when he was the Son, he learned obedience from what he suffered, and became perfect for all who obey him for the sake of eternal salvation (Heb. 5:7). But that which is progressing little by little is consummated by heresy, of which Luke also cries in the Gospel: Jesus was progressing in age, and in wisdom, and in grace (Luke 2:52). In accordance with which Paul also said: He became perfect for all who obey him for the sake of eternal salvation, called by God a high priest according to the order of Melchizedek (Heb. 5:6). Here he is compared with Moses, as to the type of leading an army; he was called the seed of Abraham, he was like his brothers in all things, he became a priest in time, he was consummated by sufferings; he who has suffered in that, himself being tempted, can help the tempted; he was called according to the order of Melchizedek the priest. So why do you feel different from Paul? Why mix the impassive God the Word with an earthly body, and make a passable priest?

Since, then, this is the only priest who sympathizes with us, and who is kindred, and who is firm, let us never be driven from his faith. For he was sent to us out of the promised blessing, from the seed of Abraham, as offering a bodily sacrifice for himself and for his race.

SERMON VII.

The fourth in Proclus. Against those who, for the sake of conjunction, either mortify the divinity of the Word, or deify humanity.

1. Indeed, I consider the insults of heretics against me as the devices of madmen, and the threatened drowning of these in the sea, also the desires of disturbances, and the news of persecutions which are aimed at the great men, and the neglect of the needy which they throw at us, and the delusions of others' chattering against us, I laugh like the noise of frogs , or at least as much as children's shooting, or camps, such as the prophet once mocked, saying: The arrows of little children have become their wounds (Ps. 63, 8).

2. But there is nothing more miserable than that shepherd, who glories in the praises of the wolves, whom if he wishes to please, and chooses to be loved by them, there will be great destruction for the sheep. Therefore, no shepherd can please wolves and flocks of sheep; Therefore, as I have said, I will despise the voices of the Lord, saying against them: You offspring of vipers, how can you say good things when you are evil (Matthew 12:34)?

3. However, it is necessary to resist and oppose these senses, with which they are armed against the Lord. For they call the mortal the vivifying Deity and dare to bring God the Word into theatrical plays, as if he were the same wrapped in cloth, and dead, alas! In order that the Lord Christ may extend his kindness to us, we are in danger of falling from the dignity of Deity with them.

4. Listen, most pitiful, and though maddened, admit to yourself the care of your health: Pilate did not kill the Deity, but the clothing of the Deity; it was not God who commanded the Word to be buried in a shroud wrapped by Joseph. For how could he suffer this, who holds the circle of the earth, and all those who dwell in it, like locusts, as the prophet says (Isaiah 40:22)?

5. But who is he who is wrapped in burial cloth? Listen to the voice of the Gospel personified: A rich man came from Arimathea, whose name was Joseph, who himself had been a disciple of Jesus. Here he went to Pilate and demanded the body of Jesus. Then Pilate ordered the body to be returned;

and taking that body, Joseph wrapped it in a clean shroud and placed it in a tomb (Matthew 27:57). He said the body three times, and not once did he mention the Deity; for the soldiers had not wounded the Deity with their lances. But what is it that is wounded by them? From John to teach: One, says he, pierced his side with his lances of the soldiers (John 19:34) And listen again to the argument by which it is established that the Deity was not at all wounded. Immediately, he says, blood and water came out (Ibid.).

6. He who gives life is not dead; for who would stand? Who would raise the dead? He comes to raise men who are dead: for he is found in the dead to help those who are lying down; not himself as lying helpless to help. God was not changed by conjunction or association with man; for it is he who cries out through the prophet: I am, I am, and I have not changed (Mal. 3:6). And again: But you are the same, and your years will not fail (Ps. 11:28). But the union of human nature and the Deity bound it up with the complexes, and raised it high, remaining what it was.

7. Therefore Peter himself, preaching about our first fruits, and recounting the height which God has contributed to this visible nature: God raised up this Jesus (Acts 10:40). Therefore, God did not die, but raised him up.

8. Hear what Peter is saying, O Apollinaris. Hear with Apollinare you also the impiety of Ariana. This, he says, God raised up Jesus; this one who dies; he whom the eyes shall behold, who was fastened to the tree, who was felt by the hands of Thomas, who cried out to him: Feel and see that the spirit has not bones and flesh, as you see me having (Luke 24:39). And being informed by these words, of the resurrection of his palpated and crucified body, he glorified God who had done these wonders: My God, saying, and my Lord (John 20:28). Not that which he had groped, calling God; for the Deity is not traced by this palpation. For if Thomas had begun to know the Word of God, or to learn by this feeling, the Lord would have said to him without a doubt: Turn up and see, for I am a spirit and God. But now from a different angle, he says, and see that I am not a spirit: for a spirit has no flesh and bones, as you see me having (Luke 24:39). Me, of course, whom you see to be composite according to what appears and appears, and according to the substance of the body you perceive to be contractible.

9. For it is not Apollinaris, the bones and flesh of the Deity of the paternal Word. Peter cries out about this palpable thing: God raised up this Jesus (Acts

10:40). Therefore, the right hand of God was exalted, but not the right hand with the help of the Word. O madness of Ariana! And by the promise of the Holy Spirit, received from the Father (Acts 2:33), he poured out this one whom you see and hear.

10. And listen to Paul reasoning about God and expounding that irreversible conjunction of God and man. He says, being constituted in the form of God, he did not presumptuously imagine himself to be equal to God; but he emptied himself, taking the form of a servant (Philippians 2:6). Thus, also in others, he says, he spoke to us in the Son, whom he appointed heir of the universe, through whom he also made the ages, who is the brightness of glory (Heb. 1:2). He calls him a son altogether, and calls him the brightness of glory, and a positive heir: a positive heir, indeed, according to the flesh; and the brightness of the paternal glory according to the Deity, because the incarnate one did not depart from the similitude which he has with the Father. For this reason also Paul says: Who is the brightness of glory; lest by any chance he should have heard any one: He was in the form of God; as if it were transitory and transitive, it would be suspected that it was of a natural nature.

11. Indeed, John, in describing the mutual co-eternity of the Word and the Father, used these sayings: In the beginning was the Word (John 1:1), He is passing away; for he did not say: In the beginning is the Word, and the Word is with God; but: In the beginning the Word was with God, and God was the Word. For it was sought what was the first existence or essence of him who made man.

12. But Paul relates all that happened at the same time, both the incarnate essence and the unchangeable and ever-abiding union of the incarnate Deity, for which reason he cried out in writing: Let this be felt in you, as also in Christ Jesus, who, when he was constituted in the form of God, emptied himself , taking the form of a servant (Philippians 2:5). He did not say: Let this be felt in you, that also in God the Word, who, when he was constituted in the form of God, took the form of a servant. But the apostle taking the name of Christ, as an appellation signifying two natures, without any danger to himself, calls him, and the form of a servant, and God irreproachable; and not only preaching this to Christians, because God Christ is unchangeable, but also kind, taking the form of a servant, and that which subsisted existing, as you know, not changed after the union, but seen at the same time kind and just: for death is his for the ungodly without the sin of the flesh; and that it

does not shrink from its enemies is an inestimable grace of kindness. For hardly, according to Paul, who should die for the righteous (Rom. 5:7)?

13. But to take up the human race through man, and to reconcile Adam, is a great circumspection of justice: for it was just that the nature which had offended should be set free once again, pleasing to God; and it is just to absolve the once burdened one who incurs the debt: for the nature of men owes to God an irreproachable and uncomplaining conduct. but he failed in the exhumation. For the negligent passions dragged the soul hither and thither, and pushed it bare of virtues, and professors of piety and justice were rare; But it was due to the entire world: for all, he says, have sinned and fall short of the glory of God (Rom. 3:23). The debt was also increasing.

14. What then is the Lord Christ? Seeing the human race bound by sin, and unworthy to be rebuked, he did not pay the debt to the government, lest justice should be injured by kindness; and Paul the Apostle, a witness of this matter, crying out: Christ, he says, whom God set forth as a propitiation through faith in his own blood for the demonstration of his righteousness (Ibid., 25); that it may be shown, he says, a just kindness, not given here and there without judgement, and in any way whatsoever: therefore Christ assumed the person of the nature of the debtor, and through it he repaid the debt as the son of Adam.

15. For it was necessary to deduct the outstanding debt from the family of him who had contracted it at one time; a debt from a woman, absolution from a woman: but learn the debt, that you may learn the retribution. Because of the meat, Adam became the debtor of the penalty. Christ solves this by starving in the desert, thwarting the plan of the devil over the provision of food.

16. He fell into the guilt of divinity against the God of appetite, when he heard from the devil: You shall be like gods (Genesis 3:5), and readily attacked the meat. But Christ redeemed this, when he promised power to the devil, for he said to him: I will give you everything, if you will fall down and worship me (Matthew 4:9), and rejecting his voice, he himself answered: Go, Satan; You shall worship the Lord your God, and serve him alone (Ibid., 10).

17. Because of disobedience in the tree of punishment, Adam was a debtor; He returned, and Christ became obedient to this on the tree (Philippians 2:8). That is why Paul also says: He took the record of our sins, which was contrary to us, from the midst, affixing it to the cross (Col. 2:14). And he who paid for us is Christ; and in him nature paid our debt. For he had assumed the person of the same nature, whose sufferings he resolved in his suffering, because we have redemption in his blood, as was said by Paul (Eph. 1:7; Col. 1:14).

18. Now see our nature in Christ pleading a cause with God against the devil and using just these allegations: I am oppressed by insults, most just judge, the devil attacks me unjustly, he uses the tyranny of impotence that is evident against me. Let it be that the former Adam gave over to death, because it was the occasion of his sin; according to Adam, whom you formed from the Virgin, for what harm, O king, did he crucify? For what reason did he hang the robbers together with him? Why is he who committed no sin, nor was deceit found in his mouth, appointed with the wicked (1 Pet. 2:22; Luke 22:37)? Or perhaps his intent to curse is not clear? Open to me like your images, O Lord. Rushing upon me without any opportunity, he endeavors to overthrow me; but you make me the just judge. You are angry with me because of Adam's transgression, for which if you have Adam without sin conjoined to you, I beg you to forgive me. For his sake you will deliver me to corruption, for his sake share in incorruption. Both of them are of my nature. As I was a partaker of the death of the former, I will become a partaker of the immortal life of the second. Undoubted and unassailable firm allegations. I will overpower my opponent. If he stirs up a dispute about the corruption that came to me from Adam, I will prescribe something different from the life of him who did not commit sin. And if he accuses me of his disobedience, I will make him guilty of his obedience.

19. Christ making this triumph over the victory of the devil: Now, he says, is the judgment of this world; now the ruler of the world will be cast out (John 12:31). For as the protoplast, the devil held guilt against all his posterity, and had an original action; thus, when he possessed the first fruits of his mass accused in Christ by his nature, when he fought against the devil, he overcame them by the very defenses of which the adversary presumed: for in Christ he most justly brings forth the accused origin of his first fruits against him, if the devil ingests the previous causes of guilt from Adam. And this is what Paul says: Christ died for our sins; indeed, he who rose again, who is at the right hand of God, also intercedes for us (Rom. 8:34).

20. For our mass clothed by Christ interpellates, completely freed from all sin, and there arises an unjust defense against our punishment, which from the beginning he who was prefigured brought upon his race: this is the opportunity of man taken up, so that man may dissolve through the flesh, rather than through the flesh He deserved corruption.

21. The burial of this man, not of the Deity, is on the third day. His feet are the key. The Holy Spirit shaped him in the womb. Concerning this flesh, the Lord said to the Jews: Loosen, he says, this temple, and in three days I will raise it up (John 2:19).

22. Do I call the double Christ alone? Does he not call himself the dissolving temple, and the raising up of the Lord? But if there was a God who was being released (which blasphemy was turned into the head of Arius), the Lord would have said: Release this God, and he will be raised in three days; if God is put to death in the tomb, Christ is lying, who said: Why do you want me to kill a man who has told you the truth (John 8:40)?

23. But Christ is not a naked man, O slanderer; but man, and God at the same time: and if God existed only, he would have had to say, according to Apollinaris: Why do you seek me to kill God, who has spoken the truth to you? But now he says: Why do you want me to kill this man who is crowned with thorns? that one who said: God, my God, why have you forsaken me (Matthew 27:46, seq.)? this one who endured death for three days?

24. And I adore this one with the Deity, as a co-operator of divine authority. For let it be manifest, says the Scripture, brethren, that the remission of sins is announced to us through Christ (Acts 13:38).

25. As if I worship the instrument of Sunday's goodness. For, he says, be kind and compassionate to one another, just as God has given us in Christ (Ephesians 4:32).

26. I honor you as a court of God's counsels: For I want you to know the knowledge of the sacrament of God the Father and of Jesus Christ, in which all the treasures of wisdom and knowledge are hidden (Col. 2:1).

27. I accept it as a guarantor for God with us. He who sent me, he says, is true, and I speak these things which I have heard from him (John 8:26).

28. I bless you as the hostage of eternal peace: for he is our peace, who made both one and the middle wall of the wall, dissolving enmities in his flesh, etc. (Ephesians 2:14).

29. Colo as propitiatory of divine indignation. God proposed Christ, he says, as the propitiatory of faith through faith in his own blood (Rom. 3:25).

30. I love and revere as mortals the beginning of immortality. For he is, he says, the head of the body of the Church, who is the beginning, the firstborn from the dead (Col. 1:18).

31. I embrace him as a mirror of the shining divinity. For God, he says, was in Christ reconciling the world to himself (II Cor. 5:19).

32. I worship the king's purple animate. For in form, he says, having been appointed by God, he emptied himself, taking the form of a servant, and was found in the habit of being a man (Philippians 2:6).

33. I praise it as the hand of the Divinity, rescuing me from death into life. For when I am lifted up, he says, I shall be from the earth, then I will draw all to myself (John 12:32). And he who is exalted, showing the faithful scribe, says: For he said this, signifying by what death he was about to die (Ibid., 33).

34. I admire it as a door to the divine entrance. For I am the door, says he; He who has entered through me will be freed, and will go in and go out and find a dwelling place (John 10:9).

35. I adore the image of the Deity as omnipotent. For God exalted him, says he, and gave him a name which is above every name, so that at his name every knee should bow of those in heaven, on earth, and in hell (Philippians 2:9).

36. I worship because of the secret that appears to the eyes. God is inseparable. I do not separate the dignity of him who protects, for it is inseparable; I separate the natures, but combine reverence.

37. That which was formed in the womb is not God by itself; God is not in himself what is created by the Holy Spirit; What is buried in a tomb is not God in itself: for thus we would be manifest worshipers of man and of the dead.

38. But since in the assumed God, from the assumed he who is assumed, as if joined to the assumed, is called God. For this reason, also the demons of the crucified flesh are horrified by the term, namely, the crucified flesh is joined to the flesh, not in proportion, knowing God. For this reason, also the judge is about to come, who appeared to me, because he is joined to the Almighty God. For then, he says, will appear the sign of the Son of man in heaven, and they will see the Son of man coming in the clouds of heaven with power and great glory (Matthew 24:30).

39. For as a king having won a victory in these states is seen with the weapons with which he overcame the enemy in war, and he wishes to be seen with them; so also the Lord King of all will come with the cross and in the flesh to his creation, to be seen with these weapons, with which he has overcome impiety, and will judge the world in the form of a man, with almighty power, according to the proclamation of Paul, who says: God, despising the times of ignorance, which are now for all men commanded to do penance; indeed he appointed the day on which he was going to judge the world in the man on whom he appointed to give faith to all, raising him from the dead (Acts 17:30). That is why it was said, so that no one should suspect a dead person to be a Deity.

40. For even if you search all the new Scriptures at the same time, you will not find anywhere in it that there is a death of God; but when it is written, to be assigned either to Christ, or to the Son, or to the Lord. For Christ, the Son, and the Lord, accepted in the Scriptures as the only begotten, is the signification of two natures; and sometimes indeed it designates Deity or humanity, sometimes both at the same time: for example, when Paul writes and preaches: We who were enemies were reconciled to God through the death of his Son (Rom. 5:10); it shows his humanity. When again he says to the Hebrews: God spoke to us in the Son, through whom he also made the

ages (Heb. 1:2); it also indicates the Deity of the Son. For the flesh is not the workman of the ages, having been fashioned after many centuries. Behold the Son of God and the Deity, and a fitting document of the appeal of the essence of humanity.

41. Let us now ask whether this name, that is, Christ, is also taken to be the Son, and this very thing pertains to the designation of both. Jesus Christ, he says, is the same yesterday and today (Hebrews 13:8). For as God existing, and man himself, according to Paul, both the last and before the ages; like a man indeed, fresh; but as God, before the ages.

42. It has been shown to you, therefore, that the appellation of Christ only shows the temple, the only God dwelling in it: demand where the Lord is also placed in the person of the Son, and now indeed that man, now God. Come, he says, see the place where the Lord was placed (Matthew 28:6). And again, the women, as if stolen by the Jews, lamenting the body of the Lord taken away: They took away, says the Scripture, my Lord (John 20:13). And Paul to the Galatians: He says, I saw no other apostle than James, the Lord's brother (Gal. 1:19). And again, he himself to the Corinthians: As often as you break this bread and drink this cup, you proclaim the Lord's death until he comes (1 Cor. 11:26). And again: Lord, as I see, you are a prophet (John 4:19). All these are documents of Dominic's incarnation, because neither was God the Word projected on the tomb. For how did he rise again, who supports the universe by the word of his power, if he lay down according to Arius? But the women did not weep for the essence of God, as if it had been stolen from the tomb. For who would suspect that the Deity could be seized by the hands of thieves? Nor again did Jacob have a brother of Divinity: nor do we announce the death of the Word of God, when we are fed with the body and blood of the Lord. For God's nature receives the sacrifice but is not itself sacrificed by the sacrifice; nor does God make prophecy, but prophecy is given, so that in this place the Lord may be, as I have said, the expression of the flesh as having the dignity of the Lord, which, however, by temperament, or admixture, has by no means passed into the substance of Deity.

43. For elsewhere the Lord is demonstrative of Deity, as it is: One God the Father, from whom all things; and one Lord Jesus Christ, through whom are all things (1 Cor. 8:6). For Christ is the maker of all things from Godhead, not from humanity, which is found after creation.

44. But elsewhere, as I said, the Lord is significant of both things, as it is: Lord Jesus, do not lay this sin on them (Acts 7:59). And: Many will say to me on that day: Lord, Lord, did we not cast out demons in your name (Matthew 7:22)? And Paul: How will the Lord, the righteous judge, repay me on that day, not only to me, but also to all who love his coming with piety (2 Tim. 4, 8). You have seen how the Christ, and the Son, and the Lord are. When the Scripture mentions the only begotten, it means only humanity, only divinity, but it wants both terms to exist.

45. Why, then, do you confuse things that are not confused? Why do you assign the name of God to death, which is never mentioned in the divine Scriptures in the commemoration of death? What Paul cried out, when you hear: In the man in whom God has determined. . . . raising him from the dead (Acts 17:31); you judge the Deity born and dead with an empty imagination.

46. But it is good that the judge will come, Paul designates this man who was visible, because the devil prepared a man shaped by God in his own image and honored with the kingdom of the earth, food for worms. Christ came according to the future in the form of a man almighty, so that even the devil himself, who with all things, was also under the dominion of God, because truly man was made in the image and likeness of God, and was appointed king of the earth and lord, rightfully the ruler of the heavens as well he reigns is brandy.

47. But your audience overcomes our conversation, and confessing that I have been overcome, I take refuge in silence, wishing always to be separated from your audience by this desire.

48 Therefore on Sunday let us celebrate the reception of humanity: let us extol the sacrament of the incarnation with incessant hymns: let us reason with God the receptive Virgin of God: let us not raise with God to the divine, I say Θεοδοχον, not Θεοτόκον, wanting to express the letter δ, not κ. For there is one, as I say according to them, Father God Θεοτόκος, that is, the begotten of God, who has this compound name. Therefore, let us depute the visible and the invisible form combined with God to be divine: an inseparable image, like a hidden image or statue of the judge. Dividing natures, let us unite honor; let us confess the double, and worship as one: for the double of natures is one according to unity.

49. If a heretic blasphemes your dead God from an ecclesiastical person, protest angrily to what has been said: It is God who raised from the dead the great Shepherd of the sheep (Heb. 13:20); he himself was not mortified, and relieved. If a Jew tells you to worship a man, answer the apostolic tradition: God was reconciling the world in Christ (II Cor. 5:19). If a Gentile pleads for the cause of accepted humanity, the remission of sins becomes an assertion. Answer him what Paul says: For by man is death, and by man is the resurrection of the dead; as in Adam all die, so in Christ all will be made alive (1 Cor. 15:21). To him be glory forever and ever.

The First Epistle of St. Cyril, bishop of Alexandria, to Nestorius

1. Venerable men and worthy of faith, coming to Alexandria, reported to us that your religion was very difficult to bear, and that you were moving everything to injure me, and relying on all means; and wishing to learn the causes of your pain, they said that certain Alexandrians had carried my letter to the holy monks, and that your hatred and disgust, being aroused against me, had caused this.

2. I wondered, then, why he did not consider your veneration more among himself, because not the first letter written by me, but certain sayings of your religion brought occasion for confusion about the faith; they are corrupted by these: for there were some who were near enough to confess that God is Christ, but rather say). But what of these is not beyond absurdity?

3. It was ours, then, to be angry at what he said, whether your religion said it or not (for I do not believe very much in the papers which are circulated). How, then, please, are we to be silent, when the right faith is wounded, and so many are being led astray every day? Shall we not stand before the judgment seat of Christ, or shall we not give account, as those appointed to speak, for our untimely silence?

4. What shall I do last? For it is time to speak, or to confer with your veneration, by asking about certain charts, which by some means were brought to Rome, by the reverend and most pious bishop of the Romans, Celestinus, with all the venerable bishops who are with him, because whether they are of your religion or not is held uncertain: for they write to us greatly offended by it.

5. By what agreement shall we satisfy even those coming from the East from all the Churches, and shall we take care of those who murmur against the same charts? Or do you think that a little disturbance arose in the Churches from these kinds of treatises? We are all anxious, and set to work to correct them, so that they may be brought back to the right path, which I do not know how to be convinced otherwise.

6. When then, your religion has brought forth the necessity and cause of these whispers, how do you think we should be justified in arguing? or by what right do you cry out against me in vain, and do not correct your speech, so that the offense of the whole world against you may cease?

7. If a speech has slipped in the plebs, it must be corrected in the treatises. Deigning to give one phrase to offended ears, the child of God, that is, Θεοτόκον pronouncing the holy virgin, that we may care for those who are clouded with sadness, holding the right glory among all regarding religion, in peace and unanimity of the group of the people.

8. But that for the faith which is in Christ we are ready to bear all things, to experience bonds and prisons, and to suffer death itself willingly, your religion does not obscure it.

9. But I say in truth that, while blessed Atticus was still established in human affairs, a book was elaborated on the holy and consubstantial Trinity, in which also a more abundant treatise on the incarnation of Dominic is contained, and it is found in harmony with what I have just written. I recited this to the bishops and clergy, as well as to the studious audience of the people; but I have published it to no one: perhaps if I publish it, I think I shall be accused again, since I composed the book even before your veneration's ordination. Salute the fraternity that is with you; those who are with us salute you in the Lord. To the most religious and holy servant Cyril, Nestorius in the Lord salutations. Indeed, nothing is more powerful than Christian modesty, nothing more steadfast. She moved us to write at present through Lampon, a very religious priest. For when he reported much of your piety, and heard much in return, he finally made no end of urging, until he obtained these things from us. For this reason, we gave up to man's importunity: for, as the matter is to be frankly confessed, the modesty of any Christian man (as in whose breast God dwells) is wont to bring me fear.

Accordingly, as regards us and ours, although not a few things have been designated by your piety as being little consistent with fraternal charity (for it is necessary to speak modestly), we are nevertheless moved to maintain a solid calmness of mind, and we have resolved to continue in the former benevolent and friendly duty of greeting by letters. But experience itself will show how far the vehement impulse of the most pious priest of Lampus is going to bring us fruit. I, and those who are with me, wish to greet the entire fraternity that is with you.

The Second Epistle of St. Cyril, bishop of Alexandria, to Nestorius

To whom Nestorius, impiously contradicting himself, thought that the same should be answered.

1. As I hear, some people talk about my reputation in your religion, and this often, taking up the opportune times of the assemblies, perhaps thinking that they would please your ears, they utter unprepared voices against us; who indeed are injured in nothing, but are reproached by us, and this gently: one who harassed the blind and the poor with injuries; the other that he had drawn a sword against his mother; thirdly, because he stole another's gold with a maid, and because has always had such a reputation as no one wished to come from, even to the most serious enemies.

2. It is true that I do not speak of such things, so that neither above my lord and teacher, nor above my fathers, the manner of pettiness which is in me should grow: for it is not easy for anyone, even though his life is circumspect, to avoid the evil curses of men, but to him by cursing and having a mouth full of bitterness (Ps. 13:3), they will sometimes render the account of all judges.

3. But let me now turn to that which best suits me; and I will remind you, even now, as a brother in Christ, of the method of doctrine and the sense of faith when preaching to the people with all caution: I will also exhort you to think that if one of those little ones who believe in Christ stumbles let the indignation of God be intolerable. But if there is a multitude of injured, how, I pray thee, should we not endeavor with all art, that offense may be prudently removed, and the reason of sound faith be insinuated to those who expound the truth?

4. Now this must be done correctly, if we read the books of the holy Fathers, and admit that they are of great importance; and proving ourselves, if we are in the faith (2 Cor. 13:5), according to what is written, let us fully and best strengthen our senses by their sayings and irreproachable definitions.

5. Therefore that holy and great council of the Fathers, the only Son begotten of God the Father by nature, but God from God, light from light, by whom

the Father created all things, came down, became incarnate, and rose again on the third day, made man, and into heaven he determined that he had ascended.

6. Now that we have known this in this way, let us see what it means that the Word of God from God was incarnate. Nor indeed do we say that God's nature was transformed and became flesh; nor because it has been changed into the whole man, who consists of soul and body: but rather we feel that God from both Christ and the Son: not that the diversity of natures is consumed by unity, but that the same natures, by an ineffable and secret concurrence to unity in Deity and humanity, make both Lord, Christ, and Son perfect one.

7. And so although he had existence before the ages, because he was born of God the Father; yet it is said that he was also born of a woman according to the flesh: not that his divine nature, in which he is consubstantial, or coessential, that is, ὁμοούσιος is to the Father, received the beginning, as it were, in the holy Virgin; nor that out of necessity for his own sake he took a second birth, after the first from the Father: for it is impious, and unskilled to feel that, to say that he did the second thing in the beginning, which existed before the ages and was coeternal with the Father, as it were; but because for our sake, and for our salvation, substantially, or essentially, united to himself as a man, he proceeded from a woman, in this way he is said to have been born also carnally.

8. For the first man did not speak of the holy Virgin. omg first] he was born, or even conceived in her, and the Word of the Father came upon him thus born; but from him and in his womb, he is believed and said to have borne a carnal birth, deputing to himself the proper birth of the same flesh.

8. Thus we say that he both suffered and rose again, not because the Word of God in his nature suffered, or felt the blows or the force of the nails, or endured the other tortures of wounds (since the Divinity is impassable, if indeed it is also incorporeal), but because, that It became his own, the body suffered, these things he himself suffered for us: for it was he who is impassive in that body that suffered.

9. In this way we also understand the dead, although he is immortal by nature, and incorruptible, and life, and the giver of life, God; but since again his own body, by the grace of God, as the Apostle Paul said, tasted death for all (Heb. 2:9); not because these things belonged to his nature (for to feel or to say this is utter madness), but because, as I said a little before, his flesh tasted death.

10. Thus also in the rising of the flesh, his resurrection is again said, not that he fell into corruption, is absent, but because that which rose again is his body.

11. Thus we confess one Christ and Lord, not as if we worshiped man together with the Word of God, lest on the occasion of one syllable, that is, the understanding or thought sneaks up on us; but as if we worship one and the same in both, because there is no body alien to the Word, with whom he sits at the right hand of the Father. Not again as two sitting sons, but as one according to unity with the flesh. For if we reject that substantial unity as either impossible or indecent, we begin to confess two sons: for it is absolutely necessary to separate them, and to say that man is indeed honored with the special term of son; But that Word of God properly owns the name of the son himself naturally.

12. Therefore, our Lord Jesus Christ is not to be divided into two sons, one and the same: for in no way does he help us to have the right reason of faith, to have this way and to feel this way; even if anyone thought to slander the unity of persons, because the Scripture did not say that the Word of God united the person to himself, but because he became flesh: but that the Word became flesh is nothing else, except because he is like us and compared, also a partaker of flesh and blood, he became ours, and made our body his own, and came forth as man.

13. On this mission, as if the reason of a sound and liquid faith is used everywhere; thus we find that the saints knew the Fathers; thus, trusting in God, they pronounced the child in labor, that is, Θεοτόκον, the holy Virgin: not that the nature of the Word of God or its Divinity took its beginning from her, as it were, but as if the rational soul had taken the body from its own animation, to whom God the Word is united according to his essence, is believed to be born according to the flesh.

14. These and such things I write out of the charity of Christ, beseeching you as a brother, and protesting in the sight of God, and exhorting the elect angels, these things you with us, and to be wise and to teach, so that peace and concord may be saved for the churches, and the bond of charity may remain indissoluble between the priests of God.

Epistle to St. Cyril, bishop of Alexandria.

To his clerics appointed in Constantinople.

1. I read the letters sent by you, in which I learned that our enemies, in meeting with you, pretended to seek peace and friendship, and to say, as I wrote to the monks, so they should keep their faith: then, looking back to their own sense, they should say the same because I myself would have said that the holy council did not remember that expression which is Θεοτόκος.

2. But I wrote that, even if the council did not put this word, it nevertheless did appropriately: for none of them had then been moved, nor was there any need to be brought into the middle, which was not in the least wanted at that time. Nevertheless, by the power and force of the understanding, I consider the mother of God, that is, Θεοτόκον, from him called the holy Virgin; for he himself says: He who was born of God the Father, through whom all things were made, was incarnate, became man, suffered, rose from the dead, ascended into heaven, and will also come to be judge.

3. Not that the Word, which according to nature was begotten of God, is to be believed to be dead, or wounded in the side by a spear (for what side does incorporeal nature have? or by what agreement is the life of lives dead?), but because this Word is united to the flesh, therefore with the patient flesh, as that is, his own body, he recalls this in himself with passion.

4. Therefore they argue and deceive themselves when they say that they want peace, and they lie to their senses: for it is easy to understand from this that they have their own virus in their hearts. They sent this deacon, who takes care of ecclesiastical affairs, two charts: one composed by Photius, or from any other, against my book which I published for the monks; and another, as it were, in the form of a quaternion, also having an inappropriate title, in this way: Against those who, because of conjunction, or Divinity, the children put to death, or they transfer humanity into God. And the preface reads as follows: The reproaches of heretics against me, etc.

5. Then they try to show that the body suffered, and not God the Word, as if, either to us or to any of those who say, that Word, which is impassive, could

have been capable of passibility. There is absolutely no one who goes mad like that; but, as we have often said, the holy council said that the very Word, by whom all things were made, suffered in his flesh, according to the Scriptures: for by his suffering body, he himself is said to have suffered, because the soul of man, since nothing in his substance and nature suffers. yet he himself is said to suffer, suffering his body.

6. But since it is their purpose to introduce two sons and two Christs: one specifically man, and the other properly God; they do only in persons, God's Word, not wanting to properly and substantially united to man-made man and man received: therefore, they turn aside, and make excuses, as it is written, in sins (Ps. 140, 4).

7. You, therefore, agreeing with them, say these things: To do them harm, because they introduce some talkative and chattering people to us, and by encouraging and defending them, they make a cause of his malignity.

8. But this is not the cause of our own injury. Say that I am not an enemy either to this one who lives there in charge; and on account of this the venerable bishops both of the East and of the West were hurt, because the doctrine of Christ was not rightly spoken, but altogether perverse.

9. Now this document is sufficient to refute them, that no such thing was ever said by anyone in the Churches, such as is contained in his expositions, which is as follows: I do not approve of your devotion to me with shouts, but I praise the desire concerning the dogmas, in which the Deity and You remember the humanity of the Lord. And after a little while: And I see that the people possess much respect and very prudent piety, but ignorance blinds them with dogmas; and this is not a crime against the common people, but, as I may say modestly or decently, because the teachers have not had time to add to you something even about the dogmas in a more clear and fluid manner.

10. Let it be said, I ask, how is it that his predecessors had no time to teach? Is John more eloquent, or is he to be compared to the blessed Atticus? Is he found to be equal to them, or wiser? What is this prouder? Or how does he not clearly confess, saying these things, that he wants to bring a new and unusual doctrine, and totally unknown to his predecessors, and this very evil, to introduce this into the Church?

11. But to me there is no word against him on other grounds: but it may happen that he repents, and at some time confesses the right faith; But concerning those things which are plotted against me, irritating and provoking my enemies, God will be satisfied.

12. But it is no wonder if the scum of the city speak ill of us, Chaeremon and Victor, and Sophronas, and the decoctioner, the servant of Flavian; for they were always around themselves, and evil towards others. But he who annoys them should know that we were never afraid to undertake a pilgrimage, but not to answer their accusations, if time demands this. For it may happen, by the dispensation of our Savior, that a council may be ordered to be called for the purpose of purifying the Church, for the lightest and most trivial reasons.

13. Therefore, that wretch will not hope, even if they still accuse us more and more worthy of faith, he would be our judge; because even if it is commanded that we should come to him, we will refute the audience of him, and with God's favor we will clarify matters more, in so far as he must satisfy his blasphemies.

14. Therefore we do not shun peace, but we also desire it, if the right faith is proclaimed and professed, or if such things finally cease to be preached at some time. For he has such perversity in his group, that it is deservedly said of those who wrote that they hold the principality in blasphemies.

15. Because it is caused, an unusual expression, to demand the mother of God, that is, Θεοτόκον, the holy Virgin, whom neither the Scripture nor the holy synod brought forth; Let him tell us, when asked, where does the Scripture speak of Christ's mother, that is, Χριστοτόκοι? Is there any episcopal council that named Christ as θεοδόχον, that is, the receiving or capable form of the deity?

16. For in that quatrain, which he sent hither, and greatly offends us, it is thus, τὴν θεοδόχον τῷ Θεῷ Λόγῳ συνθεολογῶμεν μόρφην, that is, the receptive form of God, one and equal, with which we worship God the Word, by reason of Deity. Similarly, concerning that ever-venerable Virgin, he put it this way:

17. But he does not know what he is talking about. For if the Virgin, as she wills, did not give birth to God, and is not Θεοτόκος, nor could she receive God in her womb, who is Christ, how is she at least θεοδόχος, that she may please herself again?

18. What in his sayings does he prefer to be called the Father Θεοτόκον, rather than that holy Virgin, whom he should have pronounced more correctly and competently θεογεννήτορα (the Latins would say the progenitor of God)? Let him then tell us where he read these words, or from whom he heard them. There are many accusations of his expositions, but they will be preserved, and will be brought forth in due time, unless perhaps some repentance should follow.

19. Now it is necessary for me to make my purpose clear to you, and therefore I write again, that although I am by nature peaceful and quite ignorant of disputes, yet I wish the churches to have rest, and the priests of God living in peace to be mindful of us, saying that the Lord Jesus Christ is the savior of all. My peace I give you, my peace I leave with you (John 14:27).

20. Therefore say this in your conversations, because many things have indeed proceeded from them that would injure us; nevertheless, there will be peace when he ceases to teach such things, or to feel them: for when faith is wounded, it excites enmity, and even exaggerates it.

21. If he professes the right faith, there will be a fuller and firmer peace, than if he carries it in his vow, writes the Catholic faith, and sends Alexandria: if these things are written from the affection of the innermost heart, I am also ready, for my strength, to write the like, and to publish a book. and to say that none of our priests should be burdened, because we learn that his words have a right intention and a clear purpose. If, however, he continues in the perversity of empty glory, and asks for peace, nothing remains but to oppose him with all our strength, lest we be thought to consent to him. For the faith, which is in Christ, to labor, and to live, and to die, is my greatest wish.

I have received and read the writ of execution sent to me by you, which is to be delivered to the emperor, but not without our opinion; the truth which is at length brought upon him, who acts therein, whether he is considered a brother, or by any other name, hitherto suppressed, lest he should rise up against us , he taunted that he had been brought before the emperor by us heretics. And so we dictated to him in other words, rejecting him also as our judge, in a manner of expressing enmity, and requesting that the present controversy, if they continued to be at all intrusive, be transferred to another forum. When, therefore, you have read the bill, if any necessity arises, hand it over; and if you perceive him persevering in these plots, and plotting nothing against us, carefully write them down. For I will choose pious and wise men, together with bishops, and also monks, whom I will also send to you at the earliest opportunity. For, as it is written, I will not give sleep to my eyes, nor slumber to my eyelids, nor rest to my times (Ps. 211, 4), until I am finished with the struggle for the salvation of all. Therefore, when you have now learned my opinion, act manfully. As soon as possible the letters will be prepared by me, and what they should be, and to whom they should be addressed. For I have resolved, for the sake of Christ's faith, to undergo any labor, and to endure any tortures, even those which are considered the most grievous of punishments, until I have endured so great a death, undertaken for this cause, that I am pleased with.

THE SECOND EPISTLE OF NESTORIUS.

Writing back to St. Cyril of Alexandria.

1. Indeed, the insults of your admirable letters against us, as if worthy of a remedy, I leave for patience, and for the matter and the time appropriate to answer them; but silence is not tolerated, because it brings danger if I remain silent, as I am, and I have the opportunity, to your protractedness I will try to answer the speech briefly and succinctly, shunning and declining the dark and indigestible horror of a long speech.

2. For I will begin with the wisest words of your charity, interposing them, or rather instructing them verbatim: For the Holy One, you say, and the great council, himself begotten of God the Father according to nature, the only Son, true God from true God, light from light, through whom the Father created all things, he determined that he descended, was incarnated, and became man, and suffered and rose again.

3. These are the words of your religion, and you surely recognize them as your own: hear now also us, offering a brotherly exhortation for piety, namely, this which old Paul protested to his dearest Timothy, saying: Pay attention to the lesson, to the exhortation, to the doctrine; for by doing this you will save both yourself and those who hear you (1 Tim. 4:16). What, then, tell me, does that voice want to pay attention to? Namely, reading the tradition of their saints on the surface, you did not know that there was an ignorance worthy of forgiveness for you, because you thought that they had said the Word, which is co-eternal with the Father.

4. Therefore, if you please, search these words more attentively, and you will find that the assembly of the divine Fathers did not say that the consubstantial Deity was susceptible; nor of this newly born one, who is contemporaneous with the Father; nor did she rise again, which raised the temple loose. If you will open your ears to those who offer me brotherly medicine, interposing their very voices to you, Father, I will separate you from the slander you are trying to instill in them, and through them the scriptures, I will absolve.

5. We believe, they say, and in our Lord Jesus Christ, his only begotten Son. See how the Lord, and Jesus Christ, and the only begotten Son before, shared the Deity nature, as if laying the foundations, then superimpose the tradition of the assumption of man, and of resurrection, and of passion, so that by placing certain names common and significant to both natures, they should not be dissected; nor those which are proper to the natures in the singularity of the birth of the Son, by any abolition of confusion will be endangered, in the name of union.

6. In this Paul became a teacher among them, who, when he was commemorating the divine incarnation, beginning to subjoin the things of the passions, first put Christ, the common, as I said a little before, the name of the natures; then he brings in a decent discourse or reason for both; Indeed, he says: Let this be felt in you, as also in Christ Jesus, who, when he was in the form of God, did not presumptuously think that he was equal to God. but not to one thing, which I will speak of, becoming obedient unto death, and the death of the cross (Phil. 2:5).

7. Therefore, since death had begun to be mentioned, so that no one might suspect that the Word is a passable God, Christ, as a passable and impassible essence, in the singularity of the person, put a significant term, so that the impassible and passable Christ may be called without danger: impassible indeed by Deity, but passable by nature corporeal

8. I could say many things about this, and first of all, I should be able to show that those holy Fathers only remembered not the dispensation of Divinity, but the acceptance of humanity; but I remember the brevity of the speech promised in the preface, and I feel that it restrains the conversation.

9. I come now to the second movement from your charity, in which I indeed praised the discretization of natures according to the nature of Deity and humanity, and the partnership in one person; and that you professed a Deity incapable of passion; for these things are really Catholic, and completely cut off from all things contrary to Sunday natures.

10. But in the end, if you bring to the ears of the readers some hidden, deep, and incomprehensible matter, let it be yours to examine prudence. For I know that you seemed to destroy the former things, when you brought him,

who was at first impassive, and secondly preached not to receive birth, to be again susceptible, and anew created, I know not how; It is thought by men that this very temple without sin, and inseparable from the divine nature, did not suffer birth and death for sinners; as also the voice of Dominic crying out to the Jews: Dismantle this temple, and in three days I will raise it up (John 2:19), should not be believed. He did not say: Release my Divinity, and it will be raised in three days.

11. Here again, desiring to expand my prayer, the remembrance of the promised brevity reminds me; but let me say something. Everywhere in the divine Scriptures, whenever they remember the Sunday dispensation, not the divinity of Christ, but his humanity, the passion and birth are handed down, so that according to the most liquid reason it is more suitable and suitable, the holy Virgin, not the mother of God, that is, Θεοτόκον, but the mother of Christ, that is , to be called Χριστοτόκον.

12. To these evangelists also shouting: The book of the generation of Jesus Christ, the son of David, the son of Abraham (Matthew 1:1); It is evident that God the Word was not David's son. Accept, if it seems, another testimony: And Jacob begat Joseph, the husband of Mary, of whom was born Jesus, who is called Christ (Ibid. 16). Focus on another statement: But Christ's generation was like this. When the virgin Mary was betrothed, she was found in her womb having the Holy Spirit (Ibid. 18). But who can create the Deity of the Holy Spirit of the Only Begotten or ought to be suspected? What should be poured over them? listen again: And the mother of Jesus was there (John 2:1). And again: With Mary the mother of Jesus (Acts 1:14). That also: That which is born in her is of the Holy Spirit (Matthew 1:20). And again: Take the child and his mother and flee to Egypt (Matthew 2:13). And that: Of his only begotten Son, who was made to him of the seed of David according to the flesh (Rom. 1:3). And again, about his passion: Because God sent his Son in the likeness of sinful flesh, and for sin condemned sin in the flesh (Rom. 8:3). And again: Christ died for our sins (1 Cor. 15:3). And again: I suffer Christ in the flesh (1 Peter 4:1). And that: This is my body, and this is my blood (Luke 22:19). He did not say: This is my Deity.

13. And there are ten thousand others, protesting with different and different voices, that the human race does not think that the Deity of the Son is recent, or young, or capable of bodily passions, but that flesh joined to the divine nature, from which Christ calls himself the son of David. What does he say? What do you think about Christ? Whose son is he? They answered, David.

Jesus answered and said: How then does David call him the Lord in the spirit, saying: The Lord said to my Lord: Sit at my right hand (Matthew 22:42)? It is indeed the son of David according to the flesh, but the Lord according to the Divinity. That the body of the Divinity of the Son is indeed a temple, and a temple according to some excellent and divine united conjunction, is most certain, so that it is good, and worthy of the evangelical tradition, to receive the things that are God's, and to recall to himself the divine nature.

14. But to ascribe to God the properties of the conjoined flesh, generation, and passion, and mortality, under the name of this familiarity, or to a wandering gentile, a brother, is the sense, either of the captive mind of Apollinaris and Arius, or of the rest of the plagues of heretics, and something worse than these: for it is necessary for men of this kind, attracted by the name of familiarity, and the partner of lactation for the sake of familiarity; and of the age which gradually approached, to make God the Word a partaker of the growths; and in the season of passion, from timidity, in need of angelic help.

15. I am silent about circumcision and sacrifice, and sweat, and hunger, which indeed happened to the flesh for us: yet these, when they are joined to them, are also to be worshiped; but in the Deity these are already falsely accepted, and bring to us, as slanderers, just causes of condemnation.

16. These traditions of the holy Fathers, these commandments of the holy Scriptures: thus, those who are of divine mercy and authority according to God are reasoned: Meditate on these things, be in them, that the progress may be manifest (1 Tim. 4, 15). Paul said these things to all.

17. But you do well to take care of those who are offended by us, and to have concern for those who are with us. I am grateful for your unanimity; but know that you were deceived by those who were deposed by the holy council, because of which they were filled with the disease of the Manichaeans; or what is most important, from clerics more dear to you. For the things that pertain to our Church are daily increasing for the better; and what to the people, you know to be extended to a greater extent, through the grace of Christ, to the extent that this multitude cries out with the words of the prophet: The earth will be filled with the knowledge of the Lord, as water covers many seas (Isaiah 11:9).

18. You also know how to live in a royal house, with an elucidated dogma, in great joy; and to end the page, that of the Church also with us over all the heresies that quarrel against God, see that the voice is fulfilled: Saul's house was going, and he was weak; The house of David went and was strengthened (2 Kings 3:2). These are our counsels as brother to brother; that if anyone wants to be contentious, Paul will cry out to him through us: We do not have such a custom, nor does the Church of God (II Cor. 11:16).

SERMONS VIII.

In Judah, against the heretics.

1. I would like to ask here from those heretics, who reconcile the nature of God and humanity into one essence, who is he in this place who is betrayed and handed over to the Jews. For if there was an adjustment or admixture of both, was it held by the Jews? Is God the Word, or the nature of humanity? Who seems to have been killed? For I am compelled to use lower words, so that what is said may be made manifest to all.

2. On whom, I would like you to say, do the things that have been done fall? Is it in the nature of God, which you presume to reconcile by confounding both? Therefore, the Word is a graspable God, who has nothing in common in killing with the flesh. Was he led to death by the Jews?

3. But as for what, according to you, having moderated both natures, we have recently heard the Scripture telling about the power of the sacrament, which the Lord delivered to his disciples, saying: Because in the night when it was delivered, taking the bread, giving thanks, he gave it to his disciples, saying: Take and eat all from him, for this is my body. Why did he not say: This is my Divinity, which will be broken for you? And again, why, holding out the cup, did he not say: This is my divinity, which will be poured out for you for the remission of sins; but this more: This is my blood, which will be shed for you for the remission of sins (Matthew 26:28)? Separate the nature but unite the union; To confess Christ the Son of God, but a twofold Son, man and God, so that the passion of man is indeed deputed to nature; but the absolution of passion, which was made in the man who suffered, belongs to the Divinity alone.

SERMON IX.

In what is written: If you remember that you have something against you, your brother (Matthew 5:23); as against heretics.

1. Listen intently to the words: He that eateth, saith he, my flesh, and drinketh my blood, abideth in me, and I in him. Remember that it is of the flesh, that it is said: As the living Father hath sent me, I am visible. Has the name of flesh been applied by me, so that they complain that I am misinterpreted: He who eats, says he, my flesh, and drinks my blood? Did he say: He who eats my Divinity and drinks my Divinity? but: He that eateth my flesh, and drinketh my blood, abideth in me, and I in him. And after another. But let's get to the point. He that eateth my flesh, and drinketh my blood, abideth in me, and I in him. Remember what we say about the flesh: As the living Father sent me, I who appear; but perhaps I am not interpreting correctly. Let us see from what follows: As the living Father sent me, etc.; he says of Divinity, I of humanity. Let us see who is the wrong interpreter: As the living Father sent me; the heretic says that the Divinity sent him, and that he professes to say God the Word: As the living Father hath sent me. Therefore, according to them, this should also be understood in this way: I, God the Word, live through the Father. For after this it seems to have been said: And he that eateth me liveth. Who then do we eat? Divinity or flesh?

I will also say the words of that scandal. The Lord Christ was disputing with them about his own flesh: Unless, he says, you eat the flesh of the Son of man and drink his blood, you have no life in you. Those who had heard did not understand the sublimity of the words; for they thought that, out of ignorance, they were urging him to cannibalism.

SERMON X.

As for the Macedonians, indeed for the Catholics, the defenders of the true incarnation. I have yet much to say to you, etc. (John 16:12). And after a while: The operations of the Trinity are common and can only be divided into substances. Why is the glorification of the Only Begotten sometimes attributed to the Father, as it is: My Father is he who glorifies me (John 8:54); but sometimes it is assigned to the Spirit, for he says: The Spirit of truth, who will glorify me (John 16:13); sometimes it is assigned to the power of Christ, as it is written: They went out and preached the word everywhere, cooperating with the Lord and confirming the word, following them with signs (Mark 16:16).

And the proof of this cooperation is evident: the Son became man; He placed the father on the throne; He honored the Spirit with signs; the Son dwelt in the body; the Father commended the baptized; formed in the Virgin Spirit.

SERMON XI.

Against the Arians, in these words of Isaiah: A child has been given to us, and a son has been born to us (Is. 9:6).

1. A great sacrament of such a gift; for he who appears to be a child, this who appears fresh; this one who needs corporeal bandages, this one who according to his visible essence has been recently published, is the Son, as the Scripture teaches, eternal, the Son of the creator of the universe, the Son who binds the disintegrable nature of the creature with the bandages of his help.

2. For the child is God of his own power; so far, Aries, that God the Word is under the power of God. Therefore, we know the humanity of the child and the divinity: we preserve the unity of sonship in the nature of the Deity and humanity.

3. Now I say this, that you may know how super-excellent and supreme a kind of conjunction of the Deity existed, even in the child itself, when the flesh of God was beheld; for he was himself, and the child, and the Lord of the child himself. You have praised the voice, but do not praise it too curiously; for I said that the child and the inhabitant of the child were the same.

4. So that it may be shown to them also more who it is that they adored here, and to whom the grace of the Holy Spirit led them; that is, not to the simple common sight of a child, but to a certain body ineffably joined to God.

5. Who can now look upon so vast an ocean of kindness, dominating nature with its worker, and conjoined to man the Divinity, commanding nothing without this, judging nothing without this: with him taking care of the living in supreme providence, and with him raising the dead.

The Third Synodical Epistle of St. Cyril, bishop of Alexandria.

Addressed to Nestorius, bishop of the city of Constantinople, containing twelve chapters of anathematism.

Greetings in the Lord to the religious and God-loving priest Nestorius Cyril, and to the synod of the diocese of Egypt that meets at Alexandria.

1. When our Savior declares plainly: He that loveth father or mother above me is not worthy of me; and he who loves a son or daughter more than me is not worthy of me (Matthew 10:37); What shall we suffer, who are abhorred by your religion to love you above Christ, the Savior of all? For what will it profit us in the day of judgment, or what satisfaction will we be able to find, thus keeping a long silence about the blasphemies you uttered against him? And if indeed you had only injured yourself by teaching or feeling these things, there would have been less concern for us: since indeed you have scandalized the whole Church, and stirred up the ferment of unusual corruption and new heresies among the peoples, not only being placed there, but consistent everywhere (for the books of your expositions were spread throughout they are), what is the reason beyond our silence, or is the word of apology sufficient? or how it is not necessary to remember Christ the Lord saying thus: You did not think that I came to send peace on earth, but a sword; For I have come to separate a man against his father, and a daughter against her mother (Matthew 10:34). For when faith is injured, reverence for parents is despised, as useless and dangerous, and love for children and brothers is shunned. Finally, even after life itself is chosen by pious men, so that they may achieve a better resurrection, as it is written (Heb. 11:35).

2. Behold, then, together with the holy synod, which was assembled in the great city of Rome, presided over by our most holy and most venerable brother and priest, the Celestine bishop, we have already met for the third time with these writings, giving advice to abstain from bad and distorted dogmas, which you will know both to feel and teach, but receive the correct faith handed down to the Churches by the most blessed apostles and evangelists from the beginning, who both looked with their eyes and are shown to have been ministers of the Word, know that you have no lot with us, nor can you obtain a place or a conversation with the priests and bishops of God; for it is not right to despise our Churches, a people so disturbed and

scandalized, and the most upright faith violated, dispersed without even the flock which you ought to have guarded, since you were beside us a lover of right doctrine, piously following in the footsteps of the holy Fathers. He removed from communion, or deposed from his order, laymen and clerics, we receive into our communion; for it is not right to oppress by your decrees those who know how to feel rightly, who even doing good have resisted you in the most prudent way: for this very thing you have taken care to signify in the letter which you sent to the holy proconsul of wide Rome and our co-bishop Celestinus.

5. But your religion alone is not enough to confess the symbol of faith, which was set forth at the same time, by the generosity of the Holy Spirit, by the venerable and great council assembled at Nicaea; for you did not understand this, nor did you interpret it correctly, although you uttered the same words with a perverse tone of voice. But nor is it consequent that you confess by swearing that you indeed anathematize your polluted and profane dogmas; but feel and teach what we all, whether in the East or in the West, bishops and teachers, and princes of the peoples, believe and teach. even we all, as if written correctly and irreproachably. But we have submitted to these letters of ours what you ought to feel and teach you, and from which you ought to abstain. Lord, Father Almighty, creator of all things visible and invisible. made, ὁμοούσιον to the Father, that is, of one substance with the Father, by whom all things were made in heaven and on earth; who came down for us men, and for our salvation, and was incarnated, and became man, suffered, and rising on the third day ascended into heaven, from whence he will come to judge the living and the dead. And into the Holy Spirit. There was no time when there was, and there was no time before He was born, and because He was made from no existing things, or from another substance or essence, saying that He is either a convertible and a convertible Son of God; anathematized the Catholic and Apostolic Church. coming down from the very essence of the Father, but from God, the true God, light from light, by whom all things were made, whether in heaven or on earth, for the sake of our salvation, he condescended to stoop down to empty himself, but was incarnated and became man, that is, taking the flesh of the holy Virgin, and making it his own, he sustained our birth from the womb, man proceeding from woman, and did not cast off what he was: for although he was made in the assumption of flesh and blood, yet even as he was, namely, God by nature and truth, he continued

9. We do not therefore say that the flesh was converted into the nature of the Deity, nor that the ineffable essence of the Word of God was changed into

the substance of flesh: indeed, it is unconvertible, and unchangeable, and the same Himself, according to the Scriptures, constantly permanent (Psal. 11, 28). small, but rather still in the cradles, and placed in the bosom of the maternal Virgin, he filled the whole creation as God, existing undivided from his parent: for that which is divine is known without quantity and without mass and is not contained by any boundaries. We worship one Son, the Lord Jesus Christ, not setting apart and determining man and God, as if they were one and the same united in the unity of dignity and authority; for this is the novelty of the word, and nothing else. Nor, similarly, another Christ specifically, who was born of a woman, but only one Christ, the Word of God the Father, we know with his own flesh. For then as a man, according to us, he is anointed, although he himself has contributed the Spirit of worth, but not according to the measure (John 3, 33), as the blessed evangelist John asserted. he was born of the holy Virgin, he dwelt, lest the God-man Christ the indweller should be believed to possess. Nor yet do we understand that having become flesh, as it is said to dwell in the saints, nor have we attempted to define such a dwelling made in him; but united according to nature, and not completely changed into the flesh, he made for himself such a habitation as the soul of man is believed to have in relation to his own body. having to God; for the equality of dignity alone cannot unite natures, for Peter and John are equal in dignity to each other, for which reason they are shown to be both apostles and holy disciples; yet each is not one. Nor do we notice the mode of conjunction next to collation or connection, for this is not sufficient for unity 'natural'; nor according to the effect of participation, as even we who adhere to the Lord are one spirit with him (1 Cor. 6:17). We affirm of God the Father, that we should not once more clearly divide the one Christ the Son and the Lord into two, and fall back into the crime of sacrilege, making him God of himself and Lord: for united, as we said above, God the Word in the flesh is the 'second substance', indeed God is all and ruler of the universe; nevertheless, he is neither a slave to himself, nor a master, because it is unwise, or rather impious, to feel or say this; for although he called God his Father, since God himself is also nature, and of his essence; yet we are by no means ignorant of the fact that the abiding God also became man, who would exist under God according to the due law of human nature; But how can he himself be either God or master? Therefore, as a man, as far as the measure of emptying fits decently, he argued that he is with us under God. This also just became under the law (Gal. iv, 4), although he himself promulgated the law, and the lawgiver that God may exist. again, setting him who is one into two Christs, man separately on one side, and God similarly on the other side; for he clearly denies unity, according to which one is not worshiped with another, or that God is joined together, but one is meant Christ Jesus, the only begotten Son of God, to be worshiped in one servitude with his own flesh. although according to his own nature he existed without passion, yet for us, according to the Scriptures, "He has perished in the flesh" (1 Pet. iv, 1), and he was in the crucified body of his own flesh, impassively referring to himself the passions: but the grace of God tasted death for all (Heb. 2, 9), giving him his own body, although he himself is naturally life, and the resurrection of the dead. add and he would make a way for the return of human nature to incorruption, by the grace of God, as was said above, he tasted death for all (Ibid.), and rising on the third day he plundered hell. Yet, we understand that the Word became man, which is from God, and through him the kingdom of death was destroyed (Heb. 2, 14). equity (Acts 17:31), as the Scripture testifies. for announcing according to the flesh the death of the only begotten Son of God, that is, Jesus Christ, and his resurrection, and also confessing his ascension into the heavens, we celebrate the bloodless service of sacrifice in the Churches; so also we approach the mystical blessings, and are sanctified as partakers of the body and precious blood of Christ, the Redeemer of us all, made, not as receiving common flesh, which is absent, nor as sanctified men, and joined to the Word according to the unity of dignity, or as the divine dwelling place of the possessor truly life-giving, and of the very Word of God made proper; for life naturally existing as God, because he is united to his own flesh, he professed to be life-giving. And therefore, although he says to us: Amen, amen I say to you, unless you eat the flesh of the Son of man and drink his blood (John 6:53), etc., we must not esteem her as one of us; For how can the flesh of man be vivifying according to its nature? But as truly made proper to him, who for our sakes was both made and called the Son of man. For Christ is not twofold, one and alone, although it is known that the individual has come together from two different things to unity; just as man also consists of a soul and a body, not two rather, but one of both: therefore we feel rightly observing the human and divine voices spoken by one Christ, for when he most worthy of God speaks of himself: He that seeth me seeth the Father also (John 14:9); and: I and the Father are one (John 10:30). When indeed he addresses the Jews, in no way dishonoring the measure of human nature: Now you seek me to kill the man who told you the truth (John 7:1); no less than him who in similitude and equality with the Father, we recognize God the Word even in the measure of his humanity. But if it is necessarily believed that the existing God became flesh by nature, or rather a man animated by a rational soul, what is the reason that anyone should be ashamed of their words, if he has uttered them worthy of a man? But if he rejects the words that are fitting for man, who forced him to become a man next to us? But when he mercifully inclines himself to self-emptying for our sake, for what reason did he escape the words worthy of emptying? Therefore, we ascribe to one person all his words in the Gospel, of the existence of the incarnate Word, because the Lord Jesus Christ is one, as it is written. He is continually offered to God and the Father. Again we say that he is from God according to nature, the only begotten Son, and we do not depute the name and office of the priesthood to another man besides him: for he was made a mediator of God and men, offering himself to God and the Father for us as a sweet fragrance (Eph. 2:5); and therefore he said: You did not want sacrifice and offering; burnt offerings and sacrifices for sin did not please you; but thou hast perfected a body for me. Then I said: Behold, I come; in the beginning of the book, it is written of me, that I may do thy will, O God (Heb. 10:5). for he does not need either offering or sacrifices for himself, being free from all sin, as God, existing. But if all have sinned, and stand in need of the glory of God (Rom. 3:23), according to the fact that we are more prone to the excess of changeability, and to sins human nature fell ill, but he himself did not, and therefore we need his glory; to whom will there be any more doubt that the true Lamb was sacrificed for us and for us? But he who says that he offered himself both for himself and for us, in no way escapes the crime of impiety, since he has committed absolutely nothing, and has committed no sin at all. therefore would he need an offering, without any existing deed of his own, for which, if he were, would he offer it quite appropriately? in need of glory, let us confess that we have obtained glory from the Holy Spirit, because his Spirit is neither better nor superior; but because he used the power of his own Spirit in performing wonderful works for the demonstration of his Deity, he is said to be glorified by him, just as if someone asserted of men that each one of them is enlightened by his virtue or discipline; according to that which is the Spirit, and not the Son, yet it is not alien from it; for he was called the Spirit of truth (John 16:13), and the truth is Christ (John 14:6); whence it proceedeth from him in like manner, as from God the Father. Finally, this same Spirit, performing glorious miracles also through the hands of the holy apostles, glorifies the Lord Jesus Christ, after he ascended into heaven: for Christ is believed to be God by nature, existing by his Spirit, producing virtues, and therefore he said: My God will receive it, and will announce it to you (John 16:14). However, it is not through the participation of another that the same Spirit is called wise or powerful, because it is perfect in all things, and absolutely in need of no good; for the power and wisdom of the father is believed, that is, the Son of the Spirit, and therefore the very fact and existence of virtue and wisdom are confirmed. Not that the nature of the Word's existence is the beginning of the flesh: for in the beginning was the Word, and God was the Word, and the Word was with God (John 1:1), and he is the founder of the ages, coeternal with the Father, and creator of the universe; but since, as we have said above, uniting the human nature to self-subsistence, he sustained his birth from the corporeal womb itself: not that he necessarily, because of his nature, took part in that birth, which took place in the last times of the age; but that he might bless the very first fruits of our substance, and while the woman had eaten him united to the flesh, that curse which had been pronounced against the whole human race might cease, and no longer destined our bodies for death;

also that which was said: In sorrow you will wall the children (Gen. 3:16), by dissolving himself, he would show that it was true what had been predicted by the voice of the prophet: "Death is swallowed up in victory" (1 Cor. 15:34). And again: God has taken away every tear from every face (Revelation 7:17). For this very reason we say that he dispensationally and blessed the marriage itself when he was in Cana of Galilee, when he deigned to be present with the holy apostles called. confessions supported by truth; With all these it is already agreed to agree with your religion, and apart from any trickery. However, what is necessary to anathematize your religion are subject to this letter of ours.

1. If someone does not confess that there is God, Emmanuel, and therefore the Holy Virgin, mother of God, for she gave birth according to the flesh, the Word of God made flesh, let him be anathema. man, let him be anathema.

3. If anyone in one Christ divides substances after unity, connecting them only by connection which is according to dignity, or even authority or power, and not rather by the assembly which has become natural through unity, let him be anathema.

4. If who divides into two persons or existences those words which are contained in the apostolic writings and the gospels, which are spoken of Christ by the saints, or by him even of himself, and these indeed are appropriated to a man who is specially understood apart from the Word of God; and he deputed them, as worthy of God, to the Word of God the Father alone; Let him be anathema.

5. If anyone dares to say that Christ is a man of God, that is, one who bears God, and does not rather say truly that He is God, as one Son by nature, according as the Word was made flesh (John 1:14), and shared in the same way, so that we, flesh and blood (Heb. 2, 14), be anathema.

6. If anyone says that God or the Lord Christ is the Word of God the Father, and no more confesses the same God and man at the same time, because the Word was made flesh, according to the Scriptures, let him be anathema.

7. If anyone says that Jesus is a man helped by the operation of God's Word, or ἐνεργούμενον, and to him the glory of the only begotten, as if it were given to another existing besides himself, let him be anathema.

8. And God is to be glorified and conjoined, as one with another (for with the syllables always added he forces this to be understood), and not rather that Emmanuel should be worshiped with one supplication, and one glorification depends on him, according to the fact that the Word was made flesh, let him be anathema.

9. If anyone He says that our Lord Jesus Christ was glorified by the Holy Spirit, as if he had used the power of others through him, and had received from him efficacy against unclean spirits, and the power to perform divine signs in men, and he does not rather say his own Spirit, by which he completed the divine signs. Let him be anathema.

10. The divine Scripture mentions that Christ became the priest and apostle of our confession (Heb. 3:2): And he offered himself for us as a sweet savor to God and the Father (Eph. 5:2). He says that it was done, not the Word of God itself, when it was made flesh, and man next to us, but as if another man besides himself was specially made from the woman, who knew no sin at all; let him be anathema.

11. If anyone does not confess that the flesh of the Lord is life-giving, and that it is proper to the very Word of God the Father; but as if he were joined to the same person by dignity, or as having a divine habitation, and not rather, as we have said, to be vivifying, because it became the property of the Word to vivify all things prevailing. Let him be anathema.

12. If anyone does not confess that the Word of God has passed through the flesh, and has been crucified in the flesh, and has tasted death in the flesh, and has become the firstborn from the dead, according to whom he is life and the giver of life, as God, let him be anathema.

1. I learned that the most honorable Cyril, the bishop of the city of Alexandria, because of the pamphlets presented against him to us, was frightened, and was going into hiding, in order to avoid the future sacred

synod because of these very pamphlets. the one of which he admits, but the other, in one way indeed he excludes from the Gospels, but in another way, he admits again, that is, Χριστοτόκος, according to a certain excess of prudence, I believe. to the confusion of natures, I do not resist saying to those who wish; and yet I do not doubt that this voice of Θεοτόκος should give way to that voice, which is Χριοοτόκος, as if uttered by angels and evangelists. It is known in every way to your beatitude, because if we esteem two sects opposed to each other, and the other of these utters this voice alone, Θεοτόκος; but the other only that, ἀνθρωποτόκος; and each sect shall draw the other to its own confession, so that, if it does not obtain this, it may be in danger of falling from the Church: it will be necessary for one appointed to deal with this matter, having care for both sects, to heal the danger of both parties, from the voice handed down by the evangelists, which is indicative of the nature of both For, as I have said, the word which is Χριστοτόκος moderates the assertion of these, because it also removes the blasphemy of the Samosates, which was said of Christ, the Lord of all, as a pure man. but he also flees the malice of Arius and Apollinaris.

2. Do not, then, falling short of the truth, betray it (since the letters sent to the bishops by the council of the West, and from Alexandria, were written by many to make our opinion clear to us), that is, to the prudent of the same orthodox profession; for perhaps something useful will result from the churches of the right faith, cooperating with the Lord. We salute all the fraternity.

3. And with another hand. Safe, and with a strong heart, and much praying for us, you give us, most religious brother.

4. And this I also wrote to the most honorable bishop of Alexandria, as your blessedness can know from the copies which I have attached to these letters of mine, or which were written to us by him.

5. It pleased the most pious emperors, with the Lord's adjutant, also to inexcusably indicate the synod of the whole world, because of the investigation of other ecclesiastical matters. translated by Marius Mercator.

1. Salutation to the honorable and most pious priest Celestius Nestorius in the Lord. Our age existed, the sufferings were pleasant, and indeed they were

temporary, but the truth is eternal. Thus, John the Baptist, accusing Herod of sin, and indeed the existing king, was condemned by the head: but he was not afraid, for Christ had the head, which could not be cut off. Thus, Paul and Peter were also killed in this way. And what more needs to be said?

SERMON XII.

Held in the church, in which he received the letter of denunciation from the bishop of Rome, Cyril of Alexandria, on the 7th of December, in the consulship of Theodosius XIII and Valentinian 3 Aug., the sixth day after which he received the same letter.

For it does not have the bitterness of brotherly hatred, it does not have the poison of a bruise, it does not have the rust of feigned fraternity. Such are the sweets of charity, that the Lord loves them and all. God loves charity as a good born of his kindness. And from this he instructs all nations with beneficent necessities; for since there were many things which divided the friendship of men, God inserted the undesired necessities which united them into mutual friendship. another abundance of indigenous things near the Goths; another fertility of the Spanish soil; on the other, the rich and opulent breadth of the world of Africa; for this, that what each one lacks, he takes from his neighbor; and of these, which the helpless, seeking from elsewhere, does not have, must be united in the friendship of the neighbor. Although Manichaeus was enraged a thousand times when he heard it, he did not receive this garment for natural use, but for eternal use, in order to make it at the right hand of his Divinity. He gives nothing to the living without this garment of his; He does not judge the dead without this; He willed to be one with this kingdom of his Divinity. Let Paulus of Samosate remain in stupor, who ravishes to us Sunday humanity naked from the Deity, who alone, apart from the Divinity, speaks of this which is always conjoined and connected, which is the same and equally capable as God: for God has given him a name which is above every name (Philip. 2, 9). showing from whence and whence the honor of what is seen and seen has increased: He gave him, he says, a name which is above every name, that at the name of Jesus every knee should bow, of the heavenly, earthly, and infernal, and every tongue should confess to God, because The Lord Jesus Christ is in the glory of God the Father (ibid.). For the visible and the invisible are one Son. one Christ, and he who uses, and that which he uses, two natures, but the singular Son.

4. What do you call slander? and our religion. Pius is the emperor; queens love God: be a brave man in a debate, what prevents you from entering into a debate? Why are you trying to disturb the roaring of a wild animal? do not be disturbed, since you have received the test of the Egyptian desperation of the aforesaid prophet; nor did you terrify the once blessed Flavianus, by sending letters with a tyrannical spirit; nor did you trouble Meletius, who is numbered among the saints before him. What you have you give (a good man brings

forth good things from a good treasure (Matthew 12:35), and you gave the blessed Nectarius a taste of such gifts of yours. I am silent about John, whose now I am unwillingly venerated by worshiping the ashes. I am not troubled by any concern for the episcopate, nor is there any talk of it; until I breathe, I am present with sound dogma. , he sometimes declined this voice. Many dogmas are supported by experiments, especially those of the sect of Apollinaris and of Arius, or of Eunomia. against these things which are said, so that against these things, and even the very bait which they put on the hook, you have the readiest defense. Do you know that they speak of Apollinaris? , but not according to them, you say, I utter this voice. for they are also saying Θεοτόκον, and yet, according to your confession, it is evident that they are heretics. To God and the Lord of all, they are understood to be expressed: therefore damnation to those who say, according to the sense of Apollinaris and Arius, the mother of God; and I cry together with you Θεοτόκον, but I also say Θεοτόκον, and add the mother of man, that is, ἀνθρωποτόκον; for the heretic is not permitted to say this, because of that division which has been made from the distinction of words also. for Paul also knew how to do such things, lest divisions should be made by some colored justice, when he preached grace, and confidently argued the uselessness of the law; but coming to Jerusalem, he was taught by the apostles that he should condescend to the inhabitants there, so that there would not be divisions in the Church, which seems to have the appearance of piety. What then does he do? Expounding himself in the institution of the Churches and teaching, he said: I was made to the Jews as a Jew, that I might profit the Jews; to those who are under the law, as if I were under the law, when I myself was not under the law, that I might profit those who were under the law; to those who were without the law, as if I were without the law, since I was not without the law of God, but I was in the law of Christ, that I might win those who are without the law: I became all things to all, that I might win all (1 Cor. 9:20).

9. If, therefore, you also do not, according to Apollinaris, spread the disease of Θεοτόκον to Mary, hiding the madness of Apollinaris in the person of a Catholic, confess with me what is said among all Catholics; but this is characteristic of the Catholics who utter this voice, that is, Θεοτόκον, so that they also pronounce ἀνθρωποτόκον, that is, the holy Virgin, the mother of man. the genitrix, that is, ἀνθρωποτόκος, because of the temple, which is naturally consubstantial with the Holy Virgin, although also Χριστοτόκον, that is, to say Christ's begiver, is nothing else than to confess the common thing of Divinity and humanity. And this Paul teaches, who cries of one and the same person: Jesus, he says, "Yesterday and today, he is the same for ever" (Heb. XIII, 8). For this is what Apollinaris exclaims, for this is what Arius preaches and venerates; but add the voice of the Catholics as well, which also protects

the understanding of the mother of God. which of the heretics you prudently escape, and above all the things of Paulus of Samosate, and of Photinus, which you are bound to know, you are utterly ignorant of. ; Paul and Photinus, the most imprudent of men, do not know the two natures of the Son, they do not know God and man; But they disagree with each other, and indeed with me Paul in that he says that Christ had only a man, and then only a beginning, when he was born of the Virgin. But I resist you here, so that you do not dare to make the Deity, which is eternal, contemporaneous with the flesh. or who says that the essence of the Deity in the Son was begotten of the Father before the ages? But Photinus is at this distance, not because he says the Deity is the Son, but because he says the Word is different from that which came in the last times, because he says the Word is apart from the temple. they have this difference between them: one of them says Christ only a man, while the other says indeed the Word; but he does not confess that he is God, but says that the Word is sometimes called by the name of the Father, and sometimes called by the name of the Word; whence also this he calls Λογοπατορα, that is, the Word and the Father, or, if it may be said, the Father of the Word, accepting this as his own sense of iniquity, that is well said in the Gospel: In the beginning was the Word, and the Word was with God, and God was the Word (John 1:1). But he does not introduce God the Word made man; for he does not know the Divinity of Christ, he does not know that man has assumed the divine substance, he does not know exactly the Deity of the Word existing before the ages. but this Sabellius to Photinus: because Sabellius says Υἱοπατορα the very Son who the Father, and the very Father who the Son, whereas Photinus says the Λοπατορα. But Photinus, as I said, does not have the Deity of the Word; And Sabellius indeed says the Son, but he does not say that the substance of the Son consists in property: whence he also says Υἱοπάτορα, that is, that it is the Father who is the Son, because he dreams of one substance. , he says, was the Word (John 1:1), and the rest that follow; then descending he said: And the Word became flesh (Ibid. 14); in order to show the substance of the Son existing in his own property, apart from the substance of the Father. Finally, Photinus is forced to say the Word, but the Word does not confess this Son: this Spirit foreseeing pours Himself into the heart of this writer, to fortify the souls of the Catholics. And what does he say? The Word became flesh. 17. Behold, in the meantime you have recognized the proper substance of the Word, how should we also recognize the Only Begotten, because the Father is not according to Photinus, nor the Word, but God the Word and the Son: And the Word, he says, was made flesh and dwelt in us, that is, he dwelt in our nature. And the Word became flesh, a good sign of the expression itself, so that the vanity of empty cares is taken away from every side: And the Word became flesh, he says, took on our nature. The Word, saying, was made flesh; not that he had departed from his essence, for this reason he added: And he dwelt among us; to show the indwelling of the received humanity, and the Word, he says, was made flesh. Christ has redeemed us from the curse of the law, having become a curse for us (Gal. 3:13). Surely if it were understood that what was said was changed, what was done could not give a blessing to what was cursed, could not deliver the cursed from the curse. What then is τὸ He himself took upon himself the accursed debt to us: to us, says he, sinners, the punishment of the cross was due; we remained under judicial condemnation; every kind of punishment was due to us; all the excess of punishment awaited us: but he himself came, and took on the punishment that was due to us, in innocent flesh, that he might condemn the sin itself as unjustly rushing in, crying out to the devil, the father of sin: Thieves as such as the guilty of sin you have delivered to the cross.

19. And Paul points out this, namely the condemnation of sin through Dominic's body: God, he says, sending the Son in the likeness of the flesh of sin (Rom. 8:3). Well, that in the likeness of the flesh, since the body that resembled a sinful woman was covered with the likeness of the flesh. God sent his Son, the common name of the natures, that is, of man and of God. O Ariane, it is sent according to the nature of humanity: but it is not sent according to the essence of Deity, for there is no place separated from the power of God. For in discussing this I interposed the doctrine of Paul the Apostle, showing that the Word is the Son: God sent his Son in the likeness of sinful flesh. He did not say: God sent God the Word; and certainly, the Word of God was not separate from the nature of the temple. At once, out of incompetence, they jump into a cry, saying: How did he say that there is one God the Word, and another Son who was sent? I did not say one Son, or another God the Word; but I said God the Word naturally and the temple naturally another son by conjunction one, so I also said elsewhere under the principle. do not wound me with golden arrows; I have no golden arrows. I say to you in the words of blessed Peter: I have no gold and silver; but what I have, I give you in the name of our Lord Jesus Christ of Nazareth (Acts 3:6). Learn about man and God. and man; thus and elsewhere: God sent his Son (Gal. 4:4). He did not say: God sent God the Word; for both, if he said so, would be found to be local and in part. for he who is sent is sent where he is not.

23. God sent his Son (Gal. 4:4), because it was inappropriate for the nature of Deity to be seen among those who were sent. He says, God made his Son out of a woman (Ibid.). The Son of God was born, God the Word and man: therefore she who gave birth, because of unity, is called the mother of God, that is, Θεοτόκος; because of the nature of man, the mother of man, that is,

ἀνθρωποτόκος; and since you refuse to say both in one phrase, I say God and man, do not say Χριστοτόκον (here I distinguish the voice from you only)., which is the head of our salvation.

24. God sent his Son, made of a woman, made under the law (Ibid.). Who was made under the law? The nature of the Godhead? How? did he not incur himself? The nature of the Divinity had to undertake legal purifications as well, going up into the temple to sacrifice victims? And who dared that it was the nature of Divinity?

25. Thus the Son was made under the law, and was not made: he was indeed made, received by humanity; He was not made by the majesty of the Deity; For the deity who promulgated the law, to whom else, as a lawgiver, had he to offer what are the things of the law?

26. God sent his Son, made of a woman, made under the law, to redeem those who were under the law, so that we might receive the adoption of sons. Because of this, he who knew no sin made him sin for us (Ibid.). Just like that: He was made a curse for us (Gal. 3:13). The writer has not explained to us that blessing which is the nature of the Deity turned into a curse; but because he took upon himself the sin of our nature, he signified that an unrighteous punishment rushed upon him: so also because he committed sin for us, he made him appear to the eyes of men to suffer equal criminals, and to be crucified equally with robbers. but not for himself. But for whom, O Paul? He who knew no sin made him sin for us? It was made, and he dwelt among us (John 1:14). See how he also shows the reception of man, when he says: And he dwelt among us, and we saw his glory. Whose words? One is indeed the Only-begotten, another is from the Father: therefore the Word of God is the Son. How then, Photinus, do you subvert the substance of the Divinity of the deity?

28. But if we look at the greediness of your study, here the sun itself will fail us, and perhaps we will not be able to tend to the other doctrine. So keep this with you, for the devil knows that he plans harm on men and on the good. Good discussions indeed about God; for they pour out the ointment of life in themselves, but discussions generate strife, strife stirs up anger, anger provokes hands, provoked hands move to wounds, but wounds, indeed, experience is far removed from the speech itself, what do they do, and what end do they have? .Which, indeed, to those who care for the Egyptians, will

happen in no case; for there is no room for their insolence in the city that reigns; for they have one concern, to disturb the whole everywhere. that is, a faithful discourse, so that he may be able to exhort in sound doctrine, and to rebuke those who contradict him (1 Tim. 3:2); He did not say that he is powerful to wound those who contradict him; but that he may be able to rebuke those who contradict him; and to defend sound doctrine and to embrace it. For what then if he provokes, will you be restless? It is necessary to teach those who contradict with meekness: May God never grant them to reconsider, and to repent of the snares of the devil, by which the captives are held, according to his will (2 Tim. 2, 26).

30. No one calms disturbances by disturbances; no physician heals wounds with wounds. I do not kick against a kicker; Christ was sometimes kicked, but He did not kick; but what did he say to the kicker: It is hard to kick against a spur (Acts 5:5)? Let us avert all heresy and hate Photinus with Paulus of Samosate; Let us detest the Arians with Apollinaris and let us not be troubled by the members of our own, who are implacable to every whole sect of false faith and embrace the faith of the Church. Nevertheless, they are members of the Church. And those who say only the mother of man, that is, ἀνθρωποτόκος, and these are members of the Church, but spiritually destitute of medicine. Let not fraternity rush into brothers: A brother who helps his brother will be exalted, like a firm city (Prov. 18:9) And Paul again: Brethren, he says, even if someone is preoccupied with some offense, you who are spiritual, instruct in this kind of spirit in the spirit of meekness (Gal. VI, 1).

32. Indeed, as I said, that word, that is, Χριστοτόκος, signifies two natures, both the Deity and humanity: but when dealing with simpler things, a more manifest word is needed. Say Χριστοτόκον, and Θεοτόκον and ἀνθρωποτόκον? As he who says, Christ, confesses that he is both God and man: so if you say both Θεοτόκος and ἀνθρωποτόκος, you are both confessed. and if anyone has been more impudent, let us forgive; and if anyone should speak more precisely, he shall be considered worthy of pardon in the same way. lest the humanity which has been received be imperfect. But if he brings distance in what you confess, why don't you say to him: If a statement offends my brother, I will not utter it forever. What if I seem to be less suitable to someone for the counsel of peace, hear Paul crying out to you: What you have learned, and heard, and received, and seen in me, do these things, and the God of peace will be with you (Philipp. IV, 9).

SERMON XIII.

The other day, that is, the so-called Lord's Day.

1. To others, the usefulness of other things is situated in the lands, and to some, indeed, to live in the military seems to be a great advantage; But for some it is appropriate to trade in the market of things for sale; likewise it is desirable to lend to others the study of maritime art; but the knowledge of piety in common to all men, that is to say kings and priests, popular and powerful, is useful and necessary.

2. Now what is the science of piety? If anyone wants to learn savings; for I am weary, and for you who suffer from constipation. If, then, as I said, anyone wishes to learn a summary; it is the science of piety, to enter into a correct account of the Divinity of the consubstantial Trinity, and to admit that the divine nature assumed a corporeal man. Of these things which have been frequently said, you insist, as if they had not been said, and insist vehemently on the matter of enforcement: since it is necessary to succumb to your violence, which piously possesses tyranny in us, we will repeat the same words again with you. Therefore, keep this knowledge of piety in brief.

3. But what is this, if not ὀρθολογία, and consubstantial of the divine Trinity, and assuming man of the divine nature, and conceived in the virgin womb of the flesh, and perfected man assumed by the Divinity; hence the more excellent contemplation of perfect Divinity and perfect humanity conjoined into one Son, the right of two natures into one authority fitting to the divine reason.

4. Hence we have often told you how Christ is a significant appellation of both names, that is, of humanity and of the divine nature. Hence if anyone says Christ only expressly, let him know that both natures are signified and conjoined in that name.

5. Hence the blessed Matthew, the compiler of the Gospels, when he came to the mystery of generation, made a narrative from the neutral nature of generation, but rather from the word of Christ; but it is necessary to say expressly, that the understanding may be made easier for all to see: The book,

he says, of the generation of Jesus Christ (Matthew 1:1). He did not say: The book of the generation of God's Word; nor the book of the generation of man. For if he had said, the book of the generation of man, he would have shown Christ to us only as a man. Again, if he had said, The Book of the generation of the God of the Word, he would have introduced to us a single Deity without humanity. In Christ's appeal, therefore, both natures are included, so that neither can be understood without the other.

6. Hence also to the holy Virgin, by the fact that we call her the mother-mother of Christ, we suitably appropriate the name of the twin appellation, that is, Θεοτόκος, which is the mother-mother of God, and ἀνθρωποτόκος, that is, the mother-mother of man.

7. But since it is necessary, for the sake of those who require a clearer understanding, especially since they are children of the Church, to use a more obvious expression, for that reason and in the same way that I preached briefly about that blessed Mary ever virgin, even now I proclaim with a more evident language in a loud voice, because the holy Virgin , and it is the parent of God and of man, that is, Θεοτόκος and ἀνθρωποτόκος: the parent of God indeed, because the temple which was created in it by the Holy Spirit is united to the Divinity; but the progenitor of man, because of the first fruits of our nature received from the nature of the Divinity.

8. These are the dogmas of piety in summary. Retaining these things in all things, keep them in mind, rejecting everywhere the false glory of heretics. Not as with them Θεοτόκος is a worn-out expression, so it is to be thought that the Church should also say Θεοτόκος, because neither when they say the Son, and the Church confesses the Son, the Son is equal and similar in understanding with both; but with them indeed the Son is a bare term, having nothing consubstantial with the Father; but with us the appeal of the Son is with a cause or a thing or a work. Thus, with them again the Lord of all, Christ God, is named, he is also named with us; but with them he was created, but with us he was uncreated with him who begat.

9. Therefore, from one and the same appeal, let us not be drawn into one understanding with the heretics; but let us confess that at the same time humanity and divinity were conjoined in one generation of the Son; nor by the Deity falling into the flesh, for the Divinity is unchangeable, and God, manifesting this to the Jews, said: I am, I am, and I am not changed (Mal.

3:5); nor changed by flesh through incarnation; for God is not ashamed of the nature which he has received, he is not ashamed of possessing the one who condescends to himself; for if he had been ashamed, he would not have received it. Accepted, because of the love of the human race, our nature has the unspoiled garment of Divinity. In all things possess the memory of these in Christ, to whom be glory forever and ever.

The Scriptorium Project is the work of a small group of lay people of various apostolic churches who are interested in the preservation, transmission, and translation of the works of the early and medieval church. Our efforts are to make the works of the church fathers accessible to anyone who might have an interest in Christian antiquities and the theological, philosophical, and moral writings that have become the bedrock of Western Civilization.

To-date, our releases have pulled from the Greek, Syriac, Georgian, Latin, Celtic, Ethiopian, and Coptic traditions of Christianity, and have been pulled from sundry local traditions and languages.

Other Selections from the Byzantine Church Series:

Sermons by Nestorius of Constantinople (May 2009)
Theophrastus by Aeneas of Gaza (Apr. 2011)
Treatise on Prayer by St. Evargius of Ponticus (May 2011)
The Lausiac History by St. Palladius of Galatia (Mar. 2013)
Letter on the Fall of Constantinople by Isidore of Kiev (Oct. 2013)
Selected Laws by Justinian I, Emperor of Rome (July 2018)
Exhortation to Monks Ordained in India by St. John of Karpathos (March 2021)
Fragments of 'Chronicle' by Hippolytus of Thebes (May 2023)
The Life of the Blessed Theotokos by Epiphanius Monachus (July 2023)
Letters of Nestorius by Nestorius of Constantinople (Sept. 2023)

www.ingramcontent.com/pod-product-compliance
Lightning Source LLC
LaVergne TN
LVHW052048070526
838201LV00086B/5124